Jan. 20th, 2006.

Dear Joan & Jan,

This is a little token of my gratitude for your friendship and support. I hope you'll have a great time here in Knoxville with Peter ☺.

God bless you,

Silvia R. Zinlmeier

The
NASHVILLE
Family Album

Lt. Colonel Albert and Rosemary Mayor.

To my Mom and Dad,
who put me on the edge
of a good nest,
from which I could safely fly;
and the generations
that came before them
who had no idea
that what they did
would lay the groundwork
for what I do now.
I believe in their
dreams.

The NASHVILLE *Family Album*

A COUNTRY MUSIC SCRAPBOOK

Alan L. Mayor

THOMAS DUNNE BOOKS

St. Martin's Press ✠ NEW YORK

THOMAS DUNNE BOOKS.
An imprint of St. Martin's Press.

ISBN 0-312-24412-6

Design by Susan Turner

First Edition: November 1999

10 9 8 7 6 5 4 3 2 1

CONTENTS

Thank You, Nashville

I came to Nashville at a great time. It was growing beyond its roots, and I was one of the unruly crowd attracted here to be part of it. Willie Nelson and Waylon Jennings were leading the outlaw challenge against the established concept of how to be country. Jimmy Buffett, Charlie Daniels, Dan Fogelburg, Billy Swan and Barefoot Jerry were achieving success on charts other than country. The generations seemed to be in a fight over what music should be made in this town. Thankfully, the music won.

Twenty-five years later, I see that Music City continues to attract the best of the best. I revel in the magic of a town that has showcased the talents of DeFord Bailey, Jimmie Rodgers, Uncle Dave Macon, Roy Acuff, Bill Monroe, Minnie Pearl, Hank Williams, Chet Atkins and all the other great performers of The Grand Old Opry, and now shows the world the artistry of Amy Grant, Bela Fleck, The Fairfield Four and Take Six. Great talents like Donna Summer, Steve Winwood and Kim Carnes have chosen this area as home. Everybody comes here sooner or later. I'm glad I got to move here twenty-five years ago so I could see it happen. I love this town.

I owe a debt of gratitude to many, many people both within and without the music business. My friends Diane Dickerson and Charlie Williams are at the top of the list. Their friendship throughout the years helped me in my endeavors as a citizen and a photographer. Members of several families have also been great friends throughout my time in Tennessee. They include the Adames and Morgan families in Clarksville, who have given me unconditional love and, occasionally, a couch on which to sleep when I was to pooped to drive back to Nashville. In Nashville, the Fielder and Hinsons clans have been the best friends a guy could have. Thanks for all the fun times on the Fielder Farm, where I quite often retreated to regain my sanity, and sometimes to lose it.

I especially would like to thank the Hime family here in Nashville for their love and shelter when I really needed it. To Nancy, Callie, Eamon and Kelsey, you went out of your way to take me in after the fire at my house last fall. I'm forever in your debt. I love you all. I would also like to thank Mrs. Rebekah Hanson, better known by everyone as Baba. You have been like an extra grandmother to me, enlightening me with your knowledge of Nashville's history and the wisdom that comes with a long and fruitful life. God bless you all.

There are so many people within the industry that have helped me and hired me over the years, that I don't know where to begin. My many friends at ASCAP, BMI and SESAC, and the folks at Mercury, Capitol, Curb, Sony Music, DreamWorks, Word and EMI Christian labels who have given me steady employment throughout the years. Also, the people at the various publishing companies, including Sony/Tree, MCA, Polygram, Maypop, Acuff Rose, Peer International, Island Bound, Hamstein and Patrick Joseph Music. I did a lot of work outside the industry at The Jewish Federation and The Gideons International and for photographer, Dennis Carney. I thank them for keeping me working all those years.

Thanks also goes to the many publicists who have hired me, trusting me to photograph their artists, knowing that I would do my best to make them look good. These people include Sandy Neese, Janet Rickman, Sarah Brosmer, Jerry Strobel, Evelyn Shriver, Wes Vause, Jessie Schmidt, Pam Lewis, Schatzi Hagaman, Susan Niles, Betty Hofer, Nancy Russell, Scott Stem, Karen Byrd, Nancy Henderson, Jenny Bohler, Cathy Gurley, Summer Harmon, Debbie Holley, the folks at Atkins-Muse, Sharon Allen, Sandy Brokaw, Liz Thiels, Ellen Wood, Caroline Newcomb, Eve Abdo, Michelle Goble, Rhonda Forlaw Adkins, Janet Bozeman, Craig Campbell, Shawn Williams, Joan Myers, Allen Brown, Chuck Thompson, Brenna Davenport Leigh, Greg McCarn, Lorie Lytle, Jenny Alford and many, many others.

Without the diligence of my old friend and literary manager, Harold F. Eggers, Jr., I would not be writing this book. He hooked me up with Tony Seidl at TD Media, Inc., who secured the deal with St. Martin's Press. My thanks to him and my editor, Antonia Felix, and designer, Susan Turner, who put the pieces of this puzzle together in fine fashion and with great patience. The staff at The Font Shop in Nashville also was a wonderful help in doing the final scans in record time. My thanks to Pete Wolverton at St. Martin's for understanding and accepting my suggested changes. I would also like to thank Garth Brooks and Robert K. Oermann for their friendship and participation in the project. I never realized that writing a book was such a team effort.

There are many people at various magazines that have also been a help to me by using my photos over the years. First and foremost is Music Row, with whom I've been associated for nearly fifteen years. David and Susana Ross, the staff that has varied over the years have been great friends to me, as we've watched this industry grow. Thanks to Lon Helton and the folks at Radio & Record, especially Calvin Gilbert, who supplied me with facts and figures that were instrumental in putting this book together. Thanks also to the many reporters and editors who have worked for Billboard, American Songwriter CMA's Closeup and The Tennessean throughout the years.

I have supplied photos for many fan magazines as they have gone in and out of existence since 1974. These include Country Song Roundup, Country Music, Country America, Chicago Country, Modern Screen's Country Music, KNIX Magazine and Country Weekly. Thanks goes especially to my friends Mike Greenblatt, Sandy Lovejoy, Sheldon Ivany and Neil Pond who have been among the many editors of these magazines. I'm also indebted to the photo editors at Country Weekly, Jeannie Milewski, Lisa Konicki and Summer Woods who have often requested photos from my archive, and who have understood, reluctantly, when I felt it necessary to clear some photos with clients before I released them.

Last, and certainly not least, I would like to remember my friends who won't be here to help me celebrate finishing this book. They include Helen Adames, Evelyn Dickerson, Everette Fielder, Dick Heard, Dale Franklin, Dan Wojick, Tom Davey, Otto Kitsinger and everyone's friend and mentor, Mama Mae Boren Axton. I also must remember my cat Monkey who was my sidekick for eleven years, and whose furry face has long been my logo. Their friendship and encouragement will not be forgotten by me, and should be known by all. — Alan Mayor

"It's no secret that photographers and celebrities have a history of being at war with each other, and every now and then, one of the two sides will do something to stir up the intensity even more. Alan Mayor is a breath of fresh air. Never pushy, Alan has a way of making you want to give him the good stuff. His manner is always one of respect and he's never in the way, but somehow gets the greatest shots. I'm not saying this because he's been a dear friend and he's a great guy, I'm saying it because it's the truth. When it comes to manner, respect, and humility, this celebrity could learn a lot from a photographer."

Garth Brooks

After a busy evening of shooting, as a joke, I asked my friends with Rock Solid Security to "throw me out for a photo" (1992).

I'm Not a Paparazzi !!!

Labor Day weekend 1997, I was on Center Hill Lake enjoying the woods and waters that were the first attractions that made me love Tennessee. I boated past Alan Jackson's lake house, saw Jeanne Pruett's houseboat and ate in the same marina restaurant that Kix Brooks chose for his family and friends. I thought nothing of it because that is normal if you live in a music community. I'm not the only one who loves that lake. It was 10 p.m. before I got home.

I brought a few things in and glanced at the answering machine on my way back out. The message light was blinking, so I stopped to listen before getting another load. "Alan, this is so-and-so with Channel Two News. I was referred to you about the Diana situation to get the local angle on photographing celebrities. Please call as soon as possible." I thought, "Diana who?"

I went to the next message. It was Channel 4 news: "… need to talk to you in reference to the Diana tragedy…" What? I went to the next message and discovered it was Channel 5 making the same request. All three major Nashville stations had called me and I didn't have a clue why! I had been camping or on a pontoon boat with a broken radio antenna for three days and I didn't know what they were talking about. I walked straight to the front yard and grabbed the papers, thinking there might be news of what had happened. In the back of my mind there was a little voice saying, *Right now, there's only one Diana.*

As I walked back into the house, I pulled the morning paper out of its bag, fearing what I would see. THE WORLD MOURNS THE LOSS OF A PRINCESS, read the headline. I was stunned. I scanned a few paragraphs, then, backing up a day, I ripped open the Sunday paper. CRASH KILLS PRINCESS DIANA, PAPARAZZI PURSUIT ENDS IN TRAGEDY. I read some more and went ballistic. No one would want to hear what I screamed out loud. I was angry. Someone who spent a lot of her time doing good things for the world had died, and desperate photographers were being blamed. Whether they were the cause of the accident or not, this was not the way to take photos.

I have had a rule from the very start. I do not take pictures of people to hurt them. The camera is an unforgiving, hurtful instrument in the wrong hands. Somehow, I learned that early. Maybe it was because from the beginning, I was taking photos of the friends that I had just met.

When Billy Swan had a big pop hit with "I Can Help" in 1974, I ended up across the table from him and his wife, Melva. We started talking about photography and darkrooms. A few weeks later, I went over to their house to help Melva plan a darkroom. Their VW van was in the driveway with a flat tire, and in the living room was a small Christmas tree, with a playpen underneath holding their brand-new baby. We talked about how much it would cost to set up a darkroom. Melva looked sad when I told her, but then she brightened up and said, "Oh, but with Billy's gold…" realizing the royalties would soon be rolling in. They later built a new house with a custom darkroom included. The house they left was just a few blocks away from where I live now.

I tell you this to explain how I live in this community. I don't just run in and snap a few photos and leave, I see these people daily, if not at a number-one party, then in the frozen foods at Krogers, at a kid's basketball game or in the middle of Center Hill Lake. Many of them are friends that I have known since I got here. Many of them have become my friends since they got here.

There is a sense of family in the music business. I am proud to be part of this music town, and the longer I'm here, the more protective I get of the artist's privacy. They need it to remain sane, just like every other human being on earth. They need it to make good music.

Alan L. Mayor

Foreword by Robert K. Oermann

When I arrived in Nashville in 1977—has it really been that long?—Alan L. Mayor was already "on the beat" as a photographer of the community's music makers.

I always describe the experience of coming to Music City to "make it" as like being in a school class together. Every year people arrive just like we did, in battered cars carrying threadbare possessions. Most of us come to write songs, play instruments or, heaven help us, become "stars." But Alan and I were different.

Ours was a motley class of "wanna-be's." Kathy Mattea led tours at the Country Music Hall of Fame and waited tables at T. G. I. Friday's. Steve Earle was a short order cook. Naomi Judd was putting her daughters through school by working as a nurse. Pam Tillis was singing disco songs in a motel lounge. Lots and lots of people you've probably never heard of were singing their unknown songs to each other in tiny bars. Several of them are now reasonably wealthy songwriters.

Alan and I didn't have that kind of fever. Although we were both musical, we dreamed of becoming successful documentarians. Like the others, we drank way too much beer and stayed out way too late. But neither of us lost our focus.

We "graduated" together, Alan and I. He became the dean of Nashville's freelance photographers and one of the town's most beloved characters. I worked as a journalist, wrote books and produced TV and radio shows. Today, we're fixtures on the Nashville scene, the successful "old guard" to new graduating classes of

"wanna-be's." Youngsters ask us for advice and listen to our stories about how much more fun Nashville was in the 1970's.

There's no way of knowing how many Gold-Record parties, new-artist showcases, summer concerts, #1 celebrations, nightclub happenings, arena shows, record-company and publishing-company openings, benefit events, backstage soirees, press conferences, press junkets, press receptions, artist signings and celebrity bashes that Alan and I have been to over the years. The mind reels at the thought of so many hors d'oeuvres, so many free drinks and so-o-o-o many stories. Suffice to say that whenever I arrive at any country-music event, his is the first face I look for. There is simply no other lensman in Nashville that I'd rather be shoulder to shoulder with when it's "show time."

There are a lot of reasons for that. Not the least of them is the fact that he's such a fine fellow, unfailingly good natured and enduringly kind. It goes without saying that I admire his work. My training was in fine arts and I like to think that I can spot someone with a good eye for composition. Alan has that. But, then, so do a lot of other photographers.

What I think sets his work apart is his sense of the moment. It doesn't matter if we're in a sterile modern office building on Music Row, at a broiling outdoor sweat fest, in a smoky bar or in the middle of a screaming throng of fans in an autograph line. Alan will seize that time, immerse himself in it and walk away with an image that perfectly sums it up. He will be there for the debut performance of a show-biz nobody, there for that shining time in the superstar spotlight and there for the "golden years" of a humbled legend.

And through it all, he will bring that extraordinary sense of the moment. He'll also bring the love, the caring spirit and the joy in his work that he carries with him everywhere. Count on that.

When I covered the music beat for a daily newspaper, I liked to think that I was writing contemporary history, that I was leaving behind an accurate, readable record of the times for future generations to absorb. Radio flies off into the ether, videotape decays, but words and pictures endure. Those are still what we study when we do our research into the past.

This book is a document of a community that rose to international fame as a music center in the 1970's, 1980's and 1990's. These are the faces that defined that time.

The images in these pages reflect the rise of a musical genre from a backwater substyle to a multi-million selling pop-culture phenomenon. This is a contemporary history in visual form.

This is the work of a documentarian who continues to inspire me and impress me.

This is his first book. I hope he has many more.

Meet my friend, Alan L. Mayor.

Robert K. Oermann

Robert K. Oermann

Former Pennsylvanian Robert K. Oermann is the owner of R. K. O. Products, and the best known journalist in the Nashville music business. The honesty of his reviews and interviews are both feared and respected. His writing and commentary is well known in print, on radio and television. He is also a fine graphic artist and public speaker.

As a regular columnist for Nashville's premiere music industry publication, Music Row, veteran feature writer for Nashville's newspaper The Tennessean and many others, editor-at-large for Country Music magazine and former researcher for the Country Music Hall of Fame and Archives, Mr. Oermann probably knows more about Nashville's music history than those who have lived it.

He is the author of five books, including the prestigious Women of Country Music, which he wrote with his wife, Mary Bufwack. He has written the liner notes for more than sixty albums and has written and/or produced documentaries and specials for the BBC, CMT, TBS, TNN, CBS, PBS and many others. Over the years, he has won many awards for journalism, including ASCAP's Deems Taylor Award and the CMA's Media Achievement Award. He is also a National Trustee for NARAs, best known for the Grammy Awards, and a board member for Nashville's Chamber of Commerce affiliated organization, Leadership Music.

1 | THE OLD HOMESTEAD

The Grand Ole Opry
Then and Now

This page, Garth Brooks and Roy Acuff stop for a photo outside Roy's dressing room (1992); Facing page: Jim and Jesse McReynolds harmonize on the Grand Ole Opry (1974).

With degrees in theater, English and philosophy, my chances for real-world employment were quite limited. I could become either a teacher or a stagehand. Although I had worked as a photographer while in college, I still thought I might go in other directions. As luck would have it, George Mabry, a teacher at Austin Peay State University, became the first musical director at a new Nashville theme park called Opryland USA.

In 1972, as the park was almost finished, many of the students in Austin Peay's music and theatre departments took advantage of its close proximity, only 60 miles away. We went by the carload from Clarksville to audition for performing and technical jobs that were few and far between around the area. After my tryout failed the first season, I took a choir class just so Dr. Mabry would know my name, and went back in 1973 to try out again.

This time I made it, landing the job of stage manager for the children's show called *They Went Thattaway*. I soon found out I was also the lighting and sound guy, prop-master and understudy for the lead role. As I never did learn the lead's part, I made sure he stayed healthy and was always on time. In the first few years, more than thirty-five of my college mates worked for live entertainment at Opryland USA.

It was helpful to have a nucleus of familiar faces when moving to the big city. We crashed on one another's couches, roomed together and partied together just

This page: Vince Gill, Earl Scruggs, Ricky Skaggs, Roy Husky, Jr., Marty Stuart and Alison Krauss spotlight The Opry's bluegrass tradition (1994); Facing page: Wilma Lee and Stoney Cooper sing old time country music on the new Opry stage (1974).

like we did in college—only now we were getting paid. I shared a house on 20th Avenue South with my college singing buddies, Leo Adames and Doug Sumner. That spot is now a parking lot across the street from the Sunset Grill in Hillsboro Village.

The Village was a great place for us to land. We were just a block from the Pancake Pantry, since made famous in Garth Brooks's Rolling Stone interview. The Belcourt Theatre, which was used by the *Grand Ole Opry* in the '30s when it was known as the Hillsboro Theatre, played all the current movies. There was a post office, a laundry, a small Woolworth, an H. G. Hill Market and a Third National Bank branch. The pay phone on a nearby street corner served as my communications center, and my buddies Leo and Doug lived

in the other apartment in the house. I could buy a pizza at the Villager, the neighborhood pub, and get my boots fixed, both within walking distance.

I had my first photo show at Mill's Bookstore that summer, and bought an Alverez guitar next door at Cotten Music from a salesman named Paul Worley, a Vanderbilt philosophy major who gave guitar lessons on the side to supplement his income. After years as a player, publisher and producer of artists like Martina McBride, he is now chief executive at Sony Music, overseeing the recordings of artists like Patty Loveless and Collin Raye. He just picked up his first Grammy as producer of the Dixie Chicks' album *Wide Open Spaces*. Oh, yes, he's still giving guitar lessons on the side, only now it's for W. O. Smith School of Music, where children who otherwise couldn't afford it come to take their baby steps into the music business.

Over the years, many talented people used Opryland's doors as the entryway to their dreams. A lot of us continue to have success in the Nashville music community. The summer I was there, Brooks and Dunn's producer, Don Cook, was in the country show, as was Mark Casstevens, an incredible guitarist who continues to make his mark in the studio and on the stage. Another park veteran is now head of Giant Records, home to artists Clay Walker and the

Wilkinsons. Deborah Allen, Ken Mellons and members of Diamond Rio, then known as the Tennessee River Boys, worked at Opryland as they tried to make it in Nashville.

With the closing of Opryland in 1997, Nashville lost a great source of jobs for those who dream of working in the music industry. Though Opryland still has a production company, led by fellow Austin Peay student Joe Jerles, the talent is being sent to places like Myrtle Beach, South Carolina, and Orlando, Florida, far away from Nashville's music community. One can

only hope that its replacement, Opry Mills, will be able to bring this talent back here, before they find another place they want to call home. As some country philosopher might say, "Stop up the spring and you kill the river." Time will tell.

The Grand Ole Opry

Fifty years before I got here, an institution was started quite by accident when George D. Hay introduced a live music show on WSM radio as the *Grand Ole Opry*. The name stuck, and many local performers were attracted to this showcase for down-home country music. As the 5000-watt station became a 50,000- watt clear channel station in the 1930s, the already established show was beamed into thousands of homes from the Gulf of Mexico to the Canadian provinces, from eastern cities like Pittsburgh and Roanoke, Virginia, to the Rocky Mountains, far from the little town of Nashville, Tennessee. Like a beacon, it called in talent and fans from everywhere. Soon, this new musical Mecca would come to dominate the country music market.

By the time I arrived, the show was getting ready to move into its new building at Opryland USA. In 1973, as I worked in the park, I watched the huge red brick building rise out of what had been pasture land a few years before. My first ventures into the building revealed a monstrous cavern still open below the stage, devoid of all the ropes and curtains and stage floor that would make it into a theatre. Still, I was impressed. Within a year, the new building would debut as the home of the Grand Ole Opry, and its old home, the Ryman Auditorium, would become a tourist stop.

The night they made the transition, I was hanging out with some of my new Nashville friends when a call came from a DJ, who said he had some extra tickets we could have. We knew President Nixon would be there, and security would be tight, but we decided to go anyway. We piled into my white '68 Pontiac station wagon and headed for the Opry's first night in the new building.

On the way, we saw police and roadblocks everywhere, but no one tried to stop us. As we drove up Briley Parkway, a helicopter swooped down over us, and we realized there were no other cars on the road. Just before we got to the entrance to Opryland, we found out why. There, in the other lane, heading for the airport, was the presidential motorcade. All we could do was stare in amazement as they zipped past us. Somehow, we'd gotten through security.

This page: The Grand Ole Opry is forced to perform at Nashville's Municipal Auditorium after Opryland is flooded (1975); Facing page, clockwise from top left: Connie Smith, Bluegrass legends Bill Monroe and Carl Tipton, Lorrie Morgan, Bill Monroe, Grandpa Jones, The Forester Sisters, Charlie Daniels.

Roy ACUFF

When Roy Acuff joined the Opry, he was considered part of the new sound that was changing country music. His vocals and his fiddle playing were good, but it was his ability as an entertainer that endeared him to audiences worldwide. Fans were entranced by Roy's yo-yo technique and his ability to balance his fiddle bow on his nose, skills he learned in medicine shows in his early days. With the larger venues today's superstars play, they need ropes and fireworks and banks of

This page, top to bottom: Doug Stone meets Roy Acuff before his first appearance on The Opry (1990); Roy Acuff receives the first Minnie Pearl Award, from his longtime friend, Sarah Cannon, better known as, Minnie Pearl (1989); facing page: The King of Country Music, Roy Acuff performs on the CMA's 30th Anniversary Special (1988).

Rose, where they would nurture song-writing legends like Hank Williams and others. Not only did Roy become a leader in the music community, he was even coaxed into running for governor of Tennessee in 1948. When TNN decided to have an awards show, they named the highest award after Minnie Pearl. She had the pleasure of presenting the first one to her friend, Roy Acuff.

When he passed away in 1992, Roy was mourned by all as country music's true king. I haven't heard of anyone yet who wants to take his crown.

speakers to communicate with the fans.

Acuff and Fred Rose established the powerhouse publishing company Acuff-

Shortly after his first number-one

record, Doug Stone got to perform on the *Grand Ole Opry* and was booked on the segment Roy hosted. I asked backstage if he'd ever met Mr. Acuff. Amazingly, he never had. I suggested that he go pay homage to the King.

We went to his dressing room and the two were introduced. Roy said, "You're that young fellow that's singing the song about the pine box." Doug said, "Yes, sir." "Well, I'd never sing a song like that," Roy replied.

Everyone in the room could feel

This page: Roy Acuff plays a benefit at Nashville's Municipal Auditorium (1969); facing page: Roy Acuff makes a surprise visit on Nashville Now! (1988).

Doug's discomfort. "No, at my age I'd never sing a song about dying and going to hell," Roy added. Everyone laughed. Roy continued: "Would you sing that song for me? Anybody got a guitar?" Backstage at the Opry there's probably a guitar for every 10 square feet of floor space. One was quickly handed to the nervous Mr. Stone. From a few feet away, Doug sang the entire song. I could tell that he wanted to stop after the first chorus, but Mr. Acuff stood there with his arms folded, still listening. He finished the song just in time for them to head for the stage.

With Doug's story fresh on his mind, Roy spoke highly of the "fine young man from Georgia" he'd just met backstage. Doug came out and did his new single. After the audience's applause, Roy came out and asked him to sing another song. This time, when Doug sang "I'd Be Better Off in a Pinebox," the King of Country Music stood in the shadows behind him, listening again and singing along on the choruses. There could be no better compliment for a new performer.

Thankfully, no one shot at us.

When we arrived, we found that the audience members for the second show were still standing out in the cold and beginning to get restless. Soon, someone started knocking on the glass doors, wanting to know why we couldn't come in. Someone yelled, "You let Tricky Dick in, why don't you let us regulars in?" Other sarcastic remarks followed, and someone else banged on the glass. Inside, you could see security guys scrambling and talking into their radios. Finally, after quite a delay, the doors opened and everyone headed to their seats.

It was then that we discovered why our tickets were free. The seats were in row ZZ, the very last row up in the nosebleed section. I felt like I needed a seatbelt to keep from rolling down toward the balcony. Our view of the stage was unobstructed, but Porter Wagoner was just a glimmer of sequins from there. We left early and spent forever in the parking lot, trying to find the car. I had one of those neon balls on my antenna to help me, but so did a lot of other people. I thought we would never get out of there!

A few months later, just weeks after I officially moved to Nashville, I had my second opportunity to visit the venerable hall. This time it was much more fun. A friend of mine in the park tipped me off that Paul McCartney was going to the Opry that night. I had no idea who to call, so I got into the park through people I had worked with the year before and found my way to the back door. I still had my college press card, and offered it to the guard. Though my name wasn't on the list, in the chaos, I managed to talk my way backstage.

I worked my way toward the stage and was surprised to see an opening in the curtains, center stage. I carefully peeked around the corner just in time to see Roy Acuff introduce Paul McCartney to the audience. I scrambled for my camera and took a quick shot, slightly out of focus, and discovered to my dismay that I was at the end of the roll. By the time I reloaded, the incredible moment was over.

Desperate for more photos, I went to the green room, where Paul and Linda were being interviewed. I couldn't get in, and the television reporter kept blocking me from his exclusive, so I pulled out a telephoto lens and shot between the sea of shoulders in front of me. I managed to get a few good ones and left shortly after.

I was mad at the reporter who tried to block my shots, so I called the *Tennessean* and offered my photo to them. They ran it in the Monday-morning issue, scooping the "surprise" interview that was to appear that evening on TV.

Years later, I ended up living across the street from the backstage guard, Mr. Bell, and one day confessed to him what I did. He found my story humorous, and said, "People tried things like that all the time, some got by, some didn't." He didn't remember me from Adam.

Paul McCartney is introduced to a surprised Opry audience by Roy Acuff (1974)

The Keepers of the Flame

1974 was a great time to move here. Most of the legends were still alive and drawing large audiences to the new facility. I found myself fascinated as I watched them work. Roy Acuff was the King of Country Music and Loretta Lynn charmed the audiences with songs taken from her true life experiences. Little Jimmy Dickens really was a little guy, but that only made his smile bigger, and Minnie Pearl's antics about "chasin' fellers" and Uncle Nabob brought roars of laughter from the people. Bill Monroe, with his white hat and solemn demeanor, was a commanding presence on the stage as he ripped through bluegrass numbers on his immortal Gibson mandolin.

Backstage was bustling with activity. Music came from some of the dressing rooms as bands warmed up and ran over new material. As I walked by, Loretta was giving advice to an aspiring young songwriter outside Roy's dressing room. In the green room, a woman happily gave out free coffee and lemonade. Performers opened the lockers lining the new hallways, storing their coats and getting out their instruments. People wandered casually out to the stage and watched from

This page, top to bottom: Loretta Lynn charms The Opry audience (1974); Old friends Minnie Pearl and Roy Acuff swap jokes on the Grand Ole Opry (1988); facing page: Early Opry member, DeFord Bailey performs there on his birthday (1974).

the benches behind the band. Standing in the shadows at stage right, the next act waited to go on the minute Grant Turner went to a Goo-Goo commercial. Looking at it, you'd never think there was any organization to the show at all. After years of existence, the Opry had taken on a life of its own, with the performers moving into place just in time to keep the show going. It reminded me of one of those big European clocks with the figures that always arrived just in time to ring the bell.

After photographing out there off and on for twenty-five years, I have come to realize that the passing of legends and the welcoming of new talent to the family also are part of the smooth transition that keeps the Opry running. The torch was passed from Uncle Dave Macon and DeFord Bailey to Roy and Minnie, who passed it on to Little Jimmy and Porter, who will pass it to Garth and Reba and Ricky and Vince and so on. The legends can rest easy knowing that the fire will be kept alive for generations to come, thanks to a tradition established in 1925 when George D. Hay welcomed listeners to a radio show he christened the *Grand Ole Opry*.

Welcome to the Family

Over the years, I have had the opportunity to cover many artists' first times on the *Grand Ole Opry* stage. I have always had fun witnessing these performers, from Ronnie McDowell in 1979 to Michael Peterson in 1998. The adrenaline is pumping as the young stars walk the hallways, absorbing the sights

and sounds backstage. They are just as anxious to meet the Opry veterans as any of the fans filling the seats out front. Each one is fulfilling a dream that has been inside for a for a long time, for themselves, and sometimes for their family. All of them know the significance of this moment.

Highway 101 had their first opportunity in 1988 the night after the taping of the CMA's 30th Anniversary Special. After their debut, they sought out Bill Monroe so they could have their picture made with him. Kathy Mattea made her debut in August of that same year, just a few weeks after her song "Eighteen Wheels and a Dozen Roses" made it to the top of the charts. Doug Stone found himself in Roy Acuff's dressing room, meeting the King for the first time, in 1990.

Collin Raye wanted his photo made with Connie Smith on the night of his 1992 debut. Michelle Wright got to hang out with Garth Brooks and swap stories before her 1992 performance. Randy Travis offered encouragement to Tracy Byrd in 1993, when he got his chance to make it to the Opry stage.

Deborah Allen charmed Grandpa Jones as he brought her to the stage for the first time, in the fall of 1993. She had so much fun that she came back a month later to do it again. Teen heartthrobs the Moffats invaded Porter Wagoner's dressing room in 1994 to see all the photos covering the walls. Boy Howdy and Daron Norwood also made their first appearances in 1994, and Darlye Singletary made his in 1995.

Hank Williams III made his 1996 debut wearing one of his grandfather's shirts. Some of the older artists thought they were seeing a ghost. Michael Peterson's Opry debut in 1998 was followed the next night by his first appearance on the Ryman stage at

Clockwise from far left: Young mandolin champion, Ronnie McCoury, looks on as Jesse McReynolds and Bill Monroe swap licks (1995); Grandpa Jones poses on the mock Opry stage at the Country Music Hall of Fame (1986); Garth Brooks' expression shows the joy he gets when he plays on the Grand Ole Opry (1993); Don Gibson, who wrote classics like "Oh, Lonesome Me", makes a rare Opry appearance (1994); The Four Guys, members since 1967, bring their four part harmony to the Opry stage (1988).

Bill MONROE

on the head of his mandolin while he waited to go
on. I was intrigued enough to ask someone who he
was. "That's Marty Stuart. He's only seventeen years
old," he replied. I thought to myself, *That kid wants
to be a star.*

In November of 1992, I got my answer. Press
releases announced the upcoming induction of the
Opry's next member. I called Jerry Strobel and said,
"I think you know why I'm calling, I need clearance
to come out and shoot Marty's induction." I could
hear the smile in his voice as he accepted my request.
Jerry knew that this Mississippi boy would become a
valuable connection with the traditions of country
music and its future.

He also knew that Marty cared deeply about the
responsibilities that came with officially joining the
family.

That night, it was Little Jimmy Dickens who invited the newest member to the magic circle that had
been cut from the stage of the revered Ryman
Auditorium and built into the new one at Opryland.
Backstage in the green room, under a mural created
from one of Archie Campbell's sketches, the two of
them sliced into a cake with the faces of Marty Stuart
and Lester Flatt in the icing. That cocky little kid I'd
seen seventeen years before had become a member of
the world's most important country club.

In 1995, the *Grand Ole Opry* honored one of its
most important veteran performers. After decades of
being Roy Acuff's sidekick and dobro player, Bashful
Brother Oswald was made a full-fledged member.

Known by Opry fans for his coveralls and his laugh, he
is highly respected among musicians for his skills on
the dobro. He has influenced many of today's players
with his homegrown country style. After standing in
the King of Country Music's shadow all these years, it
was only fitting for Brother Oswald to finally step into
the spotlight. Roy would have been proud of his old
friend that night.

Steve Wariner finally got his invitation in 1996 and
proudly brought his whole family along for the festiv-
ities. He had many friends in the cast, so it came as no
surprise when he was asked to join. After an introduction by Bill Anderson, Steve came to the stage to per-

What do you say about a man who created a style of playing so unique that it had to
have its own name to describe it? The
"Father of Bluegrass" was truly one of a kind.
One of the last of a generation of musicians,
he helped establish the *Grand Ole Opry* as
something more than a radio show. He influenced hundreds of musicians to try their
hand at performing. Whether they showed
up at the Opry door, at his annual Bean
Blossom Bluegrass Festival, Fanfair or other
places, they received encouragement and
honest advice.

Lester Flatt & Earl Scruggs, Ralph
Stanley, Jim & Jesse, the Osborne Brothers,
Elvis Presley, Peter Rowan, Emmylou Harris,
Steve Wariner, Ricky Skaggs, Keith Whitley,
Alison Krauss, Charlie Daniels, Bela Fleck,
Vince Gill, Marty Stuart, the Kentucky
Headhunters, Buddy Holly, Mark O'Conner,
Billy Ray Cyrus, Paul McCartney, Randy and
Gary Scruggs and literally thousands of other
musicians have a love and a livelihood that
can be traced to this man. All he asked of
people was "to play the music, take care of it,
and keep it good and clean."

Tonight, the stage goes dark for Bill

Monroe. In the last year I have noticed him
selecting one song to do by himself, accom-
panied only by his Gibson mandolin. He
chose to play for us "Poor Wayfaring
Stranger," a sad funeral dirge about going to
meet his maker. He knew the time was coming, but he didn't see any sense in waiting for
it. He continued to climb onto that stage, he
continued to advise and encourage the new
talent that sought out his blessing. Tonight all
the blessings are for Mr. Monroe. May God
bless him as He enjoys a personal performance of "Blue Moon of Kentucky." Bill
Monroe is gone, but bluegrass, his legacy,
lives on.

*This page: Bill Monroe and Ricky Skaggs buck dance dur-
ing the TV taping of the CMA's 30th Anniversary Special
(1988); facing page: Bill Monroe, the Father of Bluegrass,
shares his mandolin skills with the Opry audience (1974).*

Joe Diffie's 1st Steps charity concert. He had a hard time containing his joy as he told Diffie's audience how great his weekend had been.

But the biggest thrill for any country artist is becoming a member of the *Grand Ole Opry*. In 1986, I had my first opportunity to cover the induction of a new member. Randy Travis, the new kid from North Carolina, had swept the charts and captured the attention of the country music business, so it was not a surprise when they asked him to join. It was also not a surprise when he accepted.

Backstage, he was as nervous as a bridegroom, worrying about the awesome event that was about to occur. "Man, I am scared to death," he said to me as I congratulated him in the dressing room. I reassured him, saying, "Just remember the words, and they'll take care of the rest."

As Ricky Skaggs invited him to center stage and passed him the microphone, the Opry audience gave him a standing ovation. Randy's eyes lit up and his shy smile turned into a broad grin. When he finished singing, the fans gave him another standing ovation.

Twenty-seven-year-old Randy Traywick from Hendersonville, North Carolina, was on top of the world. He was the newest member of the *Grand Ole Opry*.

Two years later, it was time for a Pikeville, Kentucky, girl to join. With her kinship to Loretta Lynn's family and her authentic Appalachian vocal style, Patty Loveless was a natural addition to the Opry roster. In a floor- length print dress covered

with flowers and birds, she was introduced to the audience by one of her mentors, Porter Wagoner. She sang her second single, "A Little Bit of Love," which was in the top five on the radio airplay charts, and her breakthrough record, "If My Heart Had Windows." The audience loved her.

Backstage, her family crowded around as she cut the celebratory cake with the help of longtime Opry manager Hal Durham. The green room was packed with well-wishers as the cake was divided and passed around. Pink lemonade and strong coffee was available to wash it down. It wasn't very different from a wedding reception in the family living room, except that the family she was joining was one of the most famous in the world. Needless to say, she was having a great time.

In 1991, when it was Vince Gill's time to join, the King of Country Music himself, Mr. Roy Acuff, had the pleasure of introducing him to the Opry audience. Mr. Roy took great ple induction, staying on stage through mos performance. He knew how valuable a me Gill would be for the future of the Opry.

Shortly after Vince's induction, I becai about who would be next. I called Jerry S Opry's public relations director, and asked it took for an artist to become a memb *Grand Ole Opry*. "You have to want to be a and we have to want you to join." Simpl Then I asked, "When is Marty Stuart become a member?"

In 1975, on one of my first trips to the C only time I didn't take my camera), I ha intrigued by one of Lester Flatt's band membe sat on one of the benches that line the back stage, I watched as he took off his white hat an

Clockwise from far left: Randy Travis is thrilled to become a member of The Opry (1986); Longtime Opry president, Hal Durham, looks on as Patty Loveless cuts her induction cake (1988); Porter Wagoner and Marty Stuart have a lot of fun inducting Bashful Brother Oswald into the Opry after he'd been playing there with Roy Acuff since the 1940's (1995); Roy Acuff has the pleasure of inducting Vince Gill into the Opry family (1991).

form with accompaniment from his mentor, Mr. Chet Atkins. Backstage, Grandpa Jones, Jeannie Seely and Little Jimmy Dickens were among the well-wishers who welcomed him to the family.

The year 1999 brought Trisha Yearwood into the fold. Asked by Ricky Skaggs on the stage of the Ryman in January, she became a member just two months later. Half of Monticello, Georgia, came to help her celebrate this important moment in her life. With a mother who was a regular listener of the Opry and a father who believed in his daughter, Trisha had long dreamed of this night.

At the party after her first official appearance, Jeanne Pruett and ninety-year-old Bill Carlisle expressed their confidence in the future of the *Grand Ole Opry*, with artists like Trisha joining the family. They knew that the venerable institution that had asked them to join decades ago would be around for many decades to come. They looked forward to the next new member's induction. The only question was, Who would that lucky performer be? Only time would tell.

Bluegrass

I admit to being ignorant of this style of music far longer than a human being can handle. Though as a teenager I'd heard Flatt & Scruggs playing the *Beverly Hillbillies* theme at a political rally in Mississippi, I didn't know bluegrass. It was not until the Earl Scruggs Revue broke down the barriers to hipness that I really paid attention. Then I came to Nashville.

In the summer of 1973, when I worked at Opryland, they played a for few weeks within walking distance of the show that I stage managed. I would go over to see the show when I could. Earl Scruggs, of course, picked the banjo in the center, but his band consisted of Vasser Clements playing fiddle, Josh Graves working the Dobro and three kids named Randy Scruggs, Gary Scruggs and Jody Maphis rounding out the crew. I have since gotten to know the kids, and the older three are in the Bluegrass Hall of Fame. What a great introduction.

This is a style that could be called country jazz. Though there are words and a basic musical structure, most of the fire of bluegrass is in the improvisation. Bluegrass breakdowns are nothing less than some of the finest jazz I've ever heard. And it's fun, too.

In the early '80s, Ted Walker, a lawyer who was a bluegrass fanatic, began inviting pickers to his home for dinner. Some suggested that they bring their instruments along. This evolved into the Full Moon

This page, top to bottom: Bela Fleck and Edgar Meyer bring new sounds to bluegrass on the stage of The Station Inn (1985); Sister group, The McCarters, harmonize at a Full Moon Bluegrass Party (1987); facing page: Bluegrass/Jazz fiddle virtuoso, Vassar Clements, performs at The Exit In (1975).

Bluegrass Party, a spontaneous recurring event that latest over twelve years. I was privileged to attend many of these jams.

At the beginning, there would be as few as forty people there. Toward the end, the number grew to over eight hundred. Unfortunately, the party overtook the music and it had to end. But, my God, when the music was in charge, it was fabulous.

The first few years, Mark O'Conner; New Grass Revival's Bela Fleck, Sam Bush, Pat Flynn and John Cowan; Edgar Meyer, Jim Stafford, members of the Nashville Bluegrass Band; Doug Dillard, the McCarters, Peter Rowan, John Hartford, Wynonna Judd and many others attended these "pick-ins." It was a breeding ground for bluegrass. The young kids were encouraged by the masters to take the lead. Some of those kids have gone on to musical careers of their own.

Throughout the '80s and '90s, bluegrass has gained great respect. Bill's "children" have carried on his musical tradition with gusto. The Del McCoury Band, the Nashville Bluegrass Band, Ricky Skaggs and Alison Krauss have appealed to a wider audience of listeners. Mark O'Conner, Edgar Meyer and Bela Fleck have taken their bluegrass experience into the classical and jazz fields. I continue to be the happiest when I'm at a bluegrass session or listening at the Station Inn, Nashville's best place to get a bluegrass smile. ▧

Clockwise from top left: Bluegrass legend, Earl Scruggs, performs at Opryland (1973); New Grass Revival sings on the lawn for students at Vanderbilt University (1984); Cajun fiddler, Doug Kershaw, shares the stage with the award-winning fiddle/violin prodigy, Mark O'Conner (1995); Vince Gill gets to share the Opry stage with one of his heroes, Earl Scruggs (1994).

Minnie PEARL

It was February 1969 when I first crossed paths with Minnie Pearl. I had only been in Tennessee three years at that time and did not know much about her or country music. I had heard of her and Roy Acuff and the *Grand Ole Opry*, but had yet to understand what I was learning.

Having just become a Nashville visitor, I was driving out Franklin Road with some friends and my first 35mm camera, getting to know the town. Minnie Pearl's Fried Chicken had just opened and, as we drove by, we realized that she was standing in the parking lot with a camera crew doing man-on-the-street TV commercials. We pulled over to watch. Pretty soon she coaxed us over and convinced my friends to be part of one of the spots. I chose to be off camera so I could try out my new toy. Little did I know how this would foretell my future.

If anybody ever represented country music and Tennessee as well as Sarah Cannon, I have not met them. She epitomized the crossroads of country raising and city learning. Her character, Minnie Pearl, took over her life and became her vehicle out of Centerville, a small town that survived on farming and a strong family-centered life. She never changed her beliefs, she just took them to the rest of the world by the way she

Minnie Pearl brings her comedy to a taping of the TV show In Concert (1975).

lived her life as Sarah Cannon, active contributor to the Nashville community, and as the wonderful Minnie Pearl.

In the mid-'80s I covered a convention of a major food distributor at the Opryland Hotel. To make the trip interesting for their best customers, they held what was called a "mystery tour" of Nashville. The participants never knew what would happen next. One afternoon we were bussed over from the hotel to the *Grand Ole Opry* to have cocktails in front of the building. There was a bluegrass trio wandering around playing, and everyone was enjoying the wonderful spring weather. Soon someone came out of the Opryhouse and invited the group inside to see the facility.

He led us down front to a little platform in front of the stage and proceeded to enlighten us with the facts and folks that are the Opry. As he was talking about the performers, he looked up in surprise and said, "Well, look who just walked in! It's Minnie Pearl! Minnie, come over here and talk to these folks."

She bounced down the aisle to the front of the stage and proceeded to do fifteen minutes of her classic comedy, to the delight of our northern visitors. At the end of her routine, she just gushed love right back at them. "Ya'll are so sweet, I jist wish I could sit right down and have dinner with you. Come to think of it, the Opry

is my home, so why don't I just invite you to stay for dinner?" With a wave of her hand, the curtain went up and the *Grand Ole Opry* stage appeared, set up for dinner with food brought over from the hotel.

The people walked up on that stage in amazement, Minnie greeting them while they found their seats. I followed Minnie to each table so she could pose for photos with everyone there. I went through several rolls of film as she personally greeted two bus loads of people. I doubt that any of these people ever thought of her as a hick or a cornball after that.

As she left, I noticed her husband, Henry Cannon, standing in the shadows waiting for her with overcoat in hand, as he had done for forty years. As Minnie stepped out of the light and into the shadows, I saw her posture sag and noticed a stiffness that she did not have when she was onstage. She became Sarah Cannon, model citizen and loving wife. I was entranced by the transformation. I was impressed at her ability to keep performing.

People can talk about kings and queens of country music and other such royal titles based on record sales and trophies all they want. Minnie/Sarah was

Ricky Skaggs proudly poses with two of his mentors, Minnie Pearl and Roy Acuff (1987).

much more. She was the heart of country music. She epitomized the core of love and humor that empowers the musical style. Even better, she passed it on to those who follow in her footsteps. Garth and Sandy Brooks included her as part of the name of their first daughter, Taylor Mayne Pearl Brooks. Amy Grant and Gary Chapman, famed in pop and gospel, named one of their daughters Sarah after of Mrs. Cannon. All of these artists and many others honor her with their deeds, volunteering for charity work and behaving in such a way that would have made her proud. She used to say: "I'm just so proud to be here." Well, Minnie, lots of us are just so proud you were here. We miss you, and we'll never forget you. To many of us, you'll always be the heart of country music.

2 | A NASHVILLE FAMILY TREE

I remember being in a crowded record shop in Mississippi, when I was fourteen or so, looking for something worth hearing, when through the store's speakers I heard "I'm Sorry" by a youngster about my age named Brenda Lee. I was pulled into the song in a way you can never forget.

Today I heard her sing "Peace in the Valley" at the funeral of the man who produced that record. Owen Bradley, who helped create Music Row and more classic songs than I can think of right now, passed away. Floyd Cramer died a week ago, and Chet Atkins has been in ill health of late. These are people whose music made an impression on me as a teenager.

I loved Roy Orbison and Roger Miller. Chet produced the albums of a southern comedian named Brother Dave Gardner. I bought all his records. I loved Chet's work, and "Flowers on the Wall" remains one of my all-time favorites. Johnny Cash's "Ring of Fire" blew me away. Part of the thrill for me since moving here is meeting most of these people.

The Nashville Sound is often criticized, but I think that criticism is misdirected. So many people felt they had to imitate this new sound that it became overdone. As with the Urban Cowboy movement in the early '80s and the Hat Act clones of the '90s, the belief in the perfect sound gets worn out by repetition. Today though, when I hear those classics, I'm

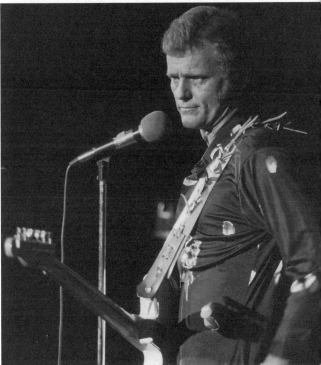

This page, top to bottom: Boxcar Willie sings a traditional country song on The Opry (1985); Jerry Reed brings his guitar and sense of humor to an early Fanfair audience (1975); facing page: Roy Orbison returns to Memphis for a performance at Libertyland (1986).

taken back to that crowded little record store in Mississippi, and I am transfixed again.

The Outlaws: Willie and Waylon

When I moved here in 1974, I had no idea who Willie Nelson and Waylon Jennings were, but then, not many people outside of Nashville and Austin, Texas, did either. When my friend, Diane Dickerson, found out, she couldn't stand my ignorance and suggested that I attend a free concert at the War

Johnny CASH

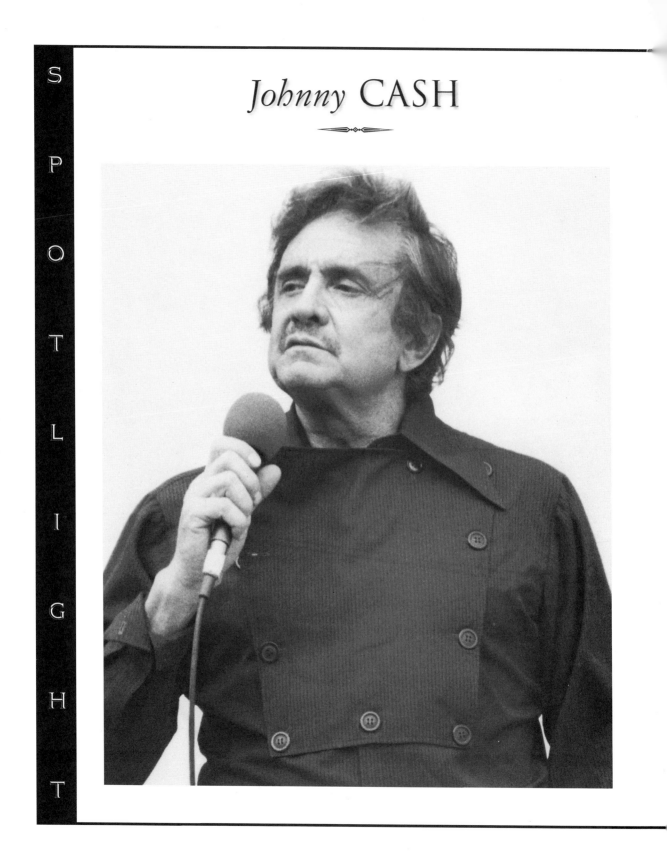

Long before I moved to Nashville, I was a Johnny Cash fan. The song "Ring of Fire," with his unique voice and Mexican horns, was a favorite of mine the minute I heard it. When I was in college, he told his fans that he would dress in black until all the war and misery in the world was ended. He refused to condemn people who were opposing the war in Vietnam and took a principled stance for peace based on American ideals and the Holy Bible. No one chose to argue with him. It only brought him respect from all sides.

He has influenced many styles of music. The folk community thought of him as one of theirs because of the rootsy, original style of music he sang. Memphis claims him as one of their rockabilly boys because he got his start there, and Nashville likes him so much they gave him five CMA awards in 1969, a record he still holds. He's in the Songwriter Hall of Fame, the Country Music Hall of Fame and the Rock and Roll Hall of Fame. His Gospel songs are soul-stirring declarations of faith that have won him respect in that field as well. He has written best-selling books. He is an American icon on a level with Roy Rogers and John Wayne, here and abroad.

I had the good fortune to attend some of the tapings for his ABC television show in the early '70s. Though it came from the Opry's Ryman Auditorium stage, his guests represented many musical styles. I

Johnny Cash grows a mustache for a made-for-TV-movie about Jesse James (1987).

saw a barefoot Linda Ronstadt mesmerize the audience with her first single, "Long, Long Time." *Bonanza*'s Lorne Green did a dramatic recitation that had everyone leaning forward in their seats. Bob Dylan and Ringo Starr were among the other superstars who came to do his show. Actor Michael Parks introduced his musical side on the show.

One night I saw Jose Feliciano do an impromptu concert between takes in the Confederate Gallery when someone yelled, "Play 'Light My Fire'!" He said he was in a bluegrass mood, then thought out loud, "Hmmm, 'Light My Fire,' bluegrass style," and ripped into it on his twelve-string guitar. The audience went wild. He grinned and started another song. Since he's blind, there was no way for the crew to signal him that it was time to resume taping. Johnny and the director, not wanting to be rude, gave up and sat down to enjoy the music. Finally, after twenty minutes, the audience reluctantly allowed the show to go on.

Johnny's regular players were exceptional talents in their own right. Mother Maybelle and the Carter Sisters and Johnny's band the Tennessee Three, the Statler Brothers, folk guitarist Norman Blake and members of the Nashville Symphony offered musical support and did their own numbers. And Johnny often did a duet with his wife, June Carter Cash. I didn't mind the waits between takes—they gave me a chance to explore the Ryman.

As an Outlaw long before the movement of the

'70s, Johnny had a profound influence on peers like Willie Nelson and Waylon Jennings and younger proteges like Kris Kristofferson. Today's performers like Travis Tritt and Alan Jackson point to his contribution. And everyone thinks it's cool to wear black.

When I asked Trisha Yearwood early in her career who her musical heroes were, she said without hesitation, "Johnny Cash. If you ever get the chance to photograph me with him, I'll love you forever!" We were at the *CMA Award Show* rehearsals.

I went out front to get an idea of the evening's schedule. After a while, Trisha came out, did "She's in Love with the Boy," then vanished behind the curtains. The next performer up was none other than the "man in black" himself. I grabbed my camera and ran backstage, where I caught up with Trisha near the dressing rooms.

"Wait right here," I said to her. She gave me a puzzled look. "There's someone coming that you want to meet." Sure enough, a couple of minutes later, here came Johnny. I introduced them and took their photo. After he left, she turned to me and said, smiling broadly, "Anything you want," then twirled around and headed for her dressing room. She's been my buddy ever since. Johnny Cash fans stick together.

Top: Johnny Cash and his daughter, Roseanne, celebrate the #1 single, "Tennessee Flat-Top Box", which he wrote in the 1950's and she recorded thirty years later (1988); Bottom: Roy Acuff stops by producer Jack Clement's studio to record a duet with Johnny Cash for his album Water From the Wells of Home (1988).

Memorial Auditorium showcasing Willie, Waylon, Johnny Paycheck and Sammi Smith. My perceptions of what could be country music were changed that night. I came out a stone-cold fan of Willie and Waylon and what would become known as the Outlaw movement.

Early in his career, Willie had been told that he couldn't sing or play guitar. Luckily, he ignored the critics and developed his own style, paying homage to influences as varied as Bob Wills and Frank Sinatra. He defied traditional guitar techniques by using a pick with a classical guitar, which accounts for the development over the years of the hole in the face of the instrument.

When his house in Ridgetop, Tennessee, caught fire, the story goes, he risked his life to save his guitar and the stash of marijuana he had hidden inside. Over the years, that guitar has been signed by the great and the relatively obscure. Even the IRS couldn't take the guitar away from him. He needed it to make a living so he could pay off his back taxes.

In the '60s, Willie tried to conform to the image that country music expected of its performers: slicked-back hair and sharkskin suits, earning the nickname "Slick Willie" long before it was used to describe a well-known politician from Arkansas. He'd already achieved tremendous success as a songwriter, with hits like "Crazy," "Night Life" and "Hello Walls," but the artists performing the songs always got the credit. It wasn't till he moved back to Texas and let his hair grow long that his career really took off. When he signed with Columbia Records in 1974, he convinced the company to let him make his own music. The result was the album *Red-Headed Stranger* and the single "Blue Eyes Cryin' in the Rain," a 1940s song written by Fred Rose, which gave him the breakthrough he needed. After all these years, Willie Nelson became a superstar overnight.

Waylon Jennings was another Texan who didn't quite fit the mold. He'd been a radio DJ in the '50s when asked to play bass by Buddy Holly, shortly before Holly's career came to its tragic end: He died in a plane crash while touring in snow-covered Iowa in 1959. Waylon was supposed to be on that flight, but gave up his seat to the legendary Big Bopper. Waylon went back to radio for a while, but soon was back on the road with his group, the Waylors.

With the help of Bobby Bare, Waylon secured a recording contract with RCA Records. He began having some success on the other side of the radio turntable, but still didn't fit in with Nashville's "metropolitan country" sound, which dominated the business at that time. Instead of trying to conform, he became even more rebellious. His music, especially in concert, was influenced by the rock and roll music he'd encountered in his early days, and he showed little concern about his appearance. His role as an outsider made him a perfect candidate for RCA Records' compilation album *Wanted: The Outlaws*, which they released in 1975, combining cuts by Willie; Waylon; Waylon's wife, Jessi Colter; and former Glaser Brother, Tom Pall. The album took off like a rocket,

WAYLON and JOHNNY
Merry Christmas and a Speedy Recovery
Your friends in Kansas and

KFDI
AM1070   FM1013

LAMAR

Left: Waylon Jennings opens for Leon Russell at the beginning of The Outlaw Movement (1974); Above: When Waylon Jennings and Johnny Cash have heart bypass surgery, a Kansas radio station pays for a get-well billboard outside their hospital. Problem was, it was facing the wrong way (1988).

bringing a whole new generation of listeners to country music.

Willie and Waylon soon found themselves being called the leaders of the Outlaw movement. Their long hair and unruly behavior was seen as a reaction to years of tailored suits and the Nashville image machine, and fit in well with the changes going on in society. Many other artists, such as Johnny Paycheck and David Allen Coe, were given more freedom as the music business adapted to this newfound popularity.

Willie and Waylon competed for a Grammy that year, with "Blue Eyes Crying in the Rain" going up against Waylon's "Are You Sure Hank Done It This Way." Willie won and Waylon didn't care. In the fall of 1975, Waylon received the CMA's Male Vocalist of the Year, and *Wanted: The Outlaws* won the CMA's Album of the Year award the following year. Waylon and Willie also took home the Vocal Duo and Single of the Year trophies, signaling the changes that were happening in Nashville. The "outlaws" were in, and designer suits were out.

Waylon and Willie's performance of "Mama's, Don't Let Your Babies Grow Up To Be Cowboys" received a Grammy in 1978, and Willie won one for his performance of "Georgia on My Mind." The CMA acknowledged his talents by giving him the Entertainer of the Year award in1979. Willie picked up more Grammys for Best New Country Song, "On the Road Again," in 1980, and another for his performance of "Always on My Mind" in 1982.

Willie's concerts were a blast. There was no telling who would join him onstage. At one show I attended in 1978, Waylon, Faron Young and gospel artist Mylon LeFevre, along with opening act Emmylou Harris and her band, which included Rodney Crowell, were onstage to sing "Will the Circle Be Unbroken" at the finale. His concerts were closer to the Grateful Dead than *Grand Ole Opry*. He even had an influence on fashion trends, with his bandannas and braided hair, and a lot of long-haired country boys thought it was OK to get their ears pierced after they noticed Willie had. The young listeners who had already been turned on by southern rock began listening to country music, the "Willie way."

Willie knew he could do good things with his newfound influence. His attempt at farming in the '60s had led him to be sympathetic to the plight of the American farmer when they started losing their farms in the early '80s. He joined forces with John Conlee, Neil Young and John Mellencamp to create Farm Aid in 1985. Many artists from Garth Brooks to Hootie and the Blowfish have helped in the cause since then.

I had the experience of covering Farm Aid VI in Ames, Iowa, in April of 1993. I was asked at the last minute, and decided to drive up from Nashville two days before rather than fly. I took the interstates to Columbia, Missouri, then headed north through the farmlands of Missouri and Iowa. On the way, I saw why the concerts were necessary: abandoned farmhouses falling down and rural towns in need of a good coat of paint. It was obvious the family farmer was hurting. By the time I got there, I understood Willie's passion.

In Iowa, April can be the cruelest month. Though the sun may be shining, the cold prairie wind will cut right through a light jacket like the one I'd brought. Soon after I got there I was at the K-Mart buying warmer clothes. Ames is a small town, so it didn't take long to find my way around. The University of Iowa's stadium, where the concert was held, was just a mile away from the hotel that became our headquarters—a mile away, that is, if you knew about the dirt road that paralleled the interstate.

Forty thousand supporters endured the cold that day to hear Willie and Neil, John and John and others from Roger Clinton to Roseanne Barr and Tom

Willie Nelson leads the troops on behalf of family farmers every-where at Farm Aid VI (1993).

Arnold. The Highwaymen, Lyle Lovett, Martina McBride, Townes Van Zandt, Jonelle Mosser and Ringo Starr were among the talents who gave their time that day.

At the end of the night, as Neil Young and Willie were working toward the finale, I looked around and realized that most of the audience was still there and getting ready to leave. I ducked out under the stage and raced for the shortcut I had found, getting to the hotel in time to watch the closing credits roll across TNN's broadcast. Then I watched traffic roll along the interstate for the next three hours.

Later that year, I had the pleasure of photographing Willie's induction into the Hall of Fame on the

Clockwise from top left: Johnny Paycheck as he looked before "Take This Job And Shove It" (1974); A fan at Farm Aid VI holds up a Jose Cuervo Willie Nelson standup in the middle of the audience (1973); The Old Dogs ride again! Mel Tillis, Waylon Jennings, Bobby Bare and Jerry Reed record several of the late Shel Silverstein's songs on a fun project which went on to receive a 1999 CMA Vocal Event of the Year nomination (1998); Willie Nelson lets his hair down (1974); Waylon Jennings plays a dying wino in Johnny Cash's video "Let It Roll" (1987).

CMA *Awards Show.* Johnny Cash, Kris Kristofferson and actor Rip Torn told why Willie was worthy of receiving such an honor. Then Willie himself came out and thanked everyone complaining that others should have been in the Hall of Fame before him. Two of the people he suggested, Merle Haggard and Ray Price, have since been inducted. The number of recipients per year has been increased to acknowledge more of the people who've made their mark on country music as it expands into the world.

Today, a whole new generation has discovered Willie and Waylon, just like they've found Johnny Cash. Though the outlaws have mellowed, the distinctive music they create continues to give young listeners new experiences. Like the outlaws of the Old West, they have moved into the folklore of music. This time though, these outlaws are considered heroes. ▣

Charlie DANIELS

S
P
O
T
L
I
G
H
T

It would be hard to call him the father of southern rock, but no other artist has cultivated it and helped it grow like Charlie Daniels. Though there are lot of incredible musicians like Dickie Betts, Toy Caldwell and the Allman Brothers, it was always Charlie who would volunteer to speak on their behalf. His song "The South's Gonna Do It Again" has become the national anthem of southern rock.

Since the early '70s, there have been seventeen Volunteer Jams, all hosted by Charlie and his band. Though Bob Dylan has never shown up, virtually everyone else has.

Since 1974, Little Richard, Billy Joel, Amy Grant, Dobie Gray, Itzhak Perlman, Carl Perkins, Ted Nugent, B. B. King, Roy Acuff, Stevie Ray Vaughn, Willie Nelson, Billy Ray Cyrus and all of the southern rock bands of legend have graced his stage—some more than once.

In 1999, Charlie took the Volunteer Jam on its first nationwide tour, with guests Molly Hatchett and the Marshall Tucker Band. It's the first time the Jam has been held outside of Nashville. And, as it has since the beginning, the Jam will use its influence to help a worthy cause—this time, Habitat For Humanity.

This page, top to bottom: Charlie Daniels hugs his special guest, B. B. King, at the Charlie Daniels Jam (1991); Charlie Daniels and his band are among the guests included when In Concert comes to Nashville to tape several shows on the Grand Ole Opry stage (1975); facing page: The Godfather of Southern Rock, Charlie Daniels (1993).

Chet ATKINS

Without the musical skills and business genius of Chet Atkins, Nashville might not have earned the title "Music City USA." Chet's skills as a guitarist can be heard on hundreds of songs recorded over the last fifty years. He is credited with influencing the dreams of thousands of musicians, from Vince Gill and Steve Wariner to Mark Knopfler, Eric Clapton and the Beatles. As an executive at RCA Records, he helped launch the careers of Elvis Presley, Willie Nelson, Dolly Parton, Ray Stevens, Charley Pride, Floyd Cramer and many others. He's had more than seventy albums in his recording career and has more awards than he can count. I started listening to him when I was about fourteen.

A few years ago, I was hired by his record label to photograph him at a guitar store forty miles away in Murfreesboro, Tennessee. I arrived at the Sony parking lot expecting to ride down with some label representatives and Mr. Atkins. When I got there, I discovered that only Chet and I would be going, and I was to drive.

Mind you, even after twenty-five years of shooting, there are some performers with whom I am still in awe. I don't know what to say to them; I just can't believe I am in their presence. Chet Atkins is at the top of the list. Not only was I going to be alone with him, I was to be responsible for his well-being for the evening.

Now, Chet is a very quiet man, and his riding

This page, top to bottom; Chet Atkins and Mark Knopfler work on the video of their award-winning recording of "Poor Boy Blues" (1990); Leona and Chet Atkins display their copy of the sign that now graces Chet Atkins Place on Nashville's Music Row (1991); facing page: Chet Atkins makes a rare appearance on the Grand Ole Opry for the induction of Steve Wariner (1996).

During the making of the video "The Claw", Jerry Reed shows Chet Atkins a new chord progression between takes (1992).

with a tongue-tied photographer certainly didn't add to the conversation. After a few snippets of small talk, he asked me if I had a tape player in the car. I did, and he produced a cassette from his pocket and asked me to play it. I popped it in, and he listened to a number by a young guitarist. Halfway through the second cut, he said, "Too repetitious—let's try this one," and handed me another tape. I put it in and a couple of cuts in, he'd heard enough to critique this guy's talent as well.

This went on all the way there and back. At one point, as I changed tapes on busy I-24, I looked up to see the spinning wheels of a semi just a few feet away from the legend. Suddenly I was terrified, real-izing one wrong move would result in newspaper headlines telling the world that Chet Atkins was killed in Alan Mayor's car. I found myself thinking, *Lord, please get us safely back to that parking lot on Music Row.* The responsibility was overwhelming.

Needless to say, we made it back, and Chet continues to have a great influence, even though he's been in poor health the last few years. Recently, when he came unannounced to the Opry's return to the Ryman in 1999, I noticed I wasn't the only one who was still in awe. As I looked around, I saw that everyone—stagehand and star, journalist and fan—was applauding the man who taught us all music, the Chet Atkins way.

3 | THE GROUPS

Staying Together

Clockwise from top left: Diamond Rio, Steve Wariner and Lee Roy Parnell makes a video of Merle Haggard's classic "Workin' Man's Blues" for the Mama's Hungry Eyes tribute album (1994); Willam Lee Golden speaks on behalf of the group when The Oak Ridge Boys are presenters on the CMA Awards not long before he was voted out of the group (1986); The Oak Ridge Boys, with new member, Steve Sanders, on the right, sign a star in a record store at the new Nashville airport (1987); The legendary Jordanaires, on the left, work with Ronnie McDowell, center, and early sidemen, D. J. Fontana and Scotty Moore, on the right, work on an Elvis tribute album (1997); Perennial favorite, Alabama, the only group to win the CMA Entertainer of the Year Award, performs on the show (1987).

The definition of *group* is "something that stays together." Unfortunately, for many, that is difficult to do. Performing in a group means you have to split up the pie among more people, making it a harder way to make a living. When Diamond Rio received its CMA award in 1997, a reporter backstage asked the boys how they keep going. Member Dana Williams replied without thinking: "Mortgages." Although Dana got a big laugh, he spoke the truth. Even when the guys are the headliners, they're making less money because they have to share. Simple economics takes a heavy toll on the longevity of groups.

Add to that the fact that you have to share the bill. Usually the group has a leader, who, not so coincidentally, almost always is also the lead singer. Randy Owen usually speaks for Alabama and makes more public appearances than his bandmates. The other guys are happy with that, and their income since the early '80s has been steady. In addition, they own Maypop Music, a very successful publishing company whose writers have supplied the group and many other artists with several major hits. They've been smart enough to know they need to stay together in order to continue their success. I wouldn't be surprised if they got some advice from the Jordanaires, who have remained the same four singers since the 1950s.

Many groups have changed group members with

varying success. When Statler Brother Lew Dewitt started having severe health problems, he was replaced by Jimmy Fortune, who had played in their band for several years. They continued their success with several more hits and a long-running TNN show. Still, when Lew's stomach problems went into remission, he was frustrated that he couldn't rejoin the group. Unfortunately, a few years later, after attempting a solo career, he succumbed to his ailment. But the Statler Brothers keep rolling on.

The Oak Ridge Boys have an equally interesting story of survival. Starting as a gospel group choir from eastern Tennessee in the 1940s, they evolved into a successful quartet that continues today. In the '80s, they had some hard times after deciding to ask William Lee Golden to leave, and replacing him with Steve Sanders. After the change, they had only one more number-one radio hit with "It's Gonna Take a Lot of River." Their fans were divided, because many sided with William Lee and were bitter about the "divorce." Unfortunately, Steve Sanders had marital and child support problems that eventually led to his dismissal from the group. Shortly after that, Duane, Richard and Joe invited William Lee to rejoin them, which brought renewed success. Sadly, in 1998, Steve Sanders committed suicide after several attempts at starting a solo career. But the Oak Ridge Boys keep rolling on.

In the late '80s, at a talent buyers convention, I ended up at a breakfast table with Clarence Spalding (now part of Titley/Spalding Management, with Brooks & Dunn, Kathy Mattea and Chely Wright). At

that time he was working with the ever changing group Exile. He was frustrated with club owners who pointed out that the marquee photo differed from the group that actually showed up. They didn't want to pay, saying, "This isn't the group we booked." Today, Les Taylor and J. P. Pennington, two of the original members, own the name and continue to tour as Exile.

Other groups, like the Glaser Brothers, Highway 101, Restless Heart, Little Texas, The Kentucky Headhunters and Shenandoah, suffered when members decided to break out on their own. Sawyer Brown had one member leave to pursue TV ventures, but suffered few side effects. After John McCuen left the Nitty Gritty Dirt Band, their careers continued to thrive, as did his solo career. Many groups fell apart because of simple economics: too many mouths and not enough pie.

New Grass Revival, my favorite group of all time (next to the Beatles and Crosby, Stills, Nash & Young), hit an artistic plateau but couldn't make it up the mountain to major stardom. They split up amicably to pursue individual projects. Bela Fleck now has the Flecktones, who are consistently winning jazz

Clockwise from top left; The Kentucky Headhunters run into Ronnie McDowell at the Country Radio Seminar. Fred and Richard Young, on the left, and their cousin, Greg Martin, in the center, worked in Ronnie's band in the mid-80's. Brothers Ricky Lee and Doug Phelps, on the right, later joined the band that would win two CMA Vocal Group of the Year awards (1991); The members of Highway 101 get to meet Bill Monroe on the night of their debut on the Grand Ole Opry (1988); Shenandoah celebrates its first #1 with the writers of "Church on Cumberland Road", Bob DePiero, John Scott Sherrill and Dennis Robbins, in the center. The writers would later have their own group called Billy Hill (1989); The group, Sawyer Brown, who won the 1985 CMA Horizon Award, make an appearance on the show (1987); The Mavericks don tuxedos for member, Robert Reynolds', wedding to Trisha Yearwood (1994).

awards, including another Grammy in 1999. Sam Bush won a Grammy as a member of the Nash Ramblers, Emmylou Harris's band for several years. He recently had two highly acclaimed solo albums.

John Cowan was in the Sky Kings for the short time they existed and continues with solo projects. Pat Flynn is a sought-after session player and producer. But inside the industry, the Sky Kings continue to be elevated to legend status. Rounder Records continues to sell albums they recorded for them in the '80s. When Garth Brooks decided to record "Callin' Baton Rouge," which was their last radio single, he asked the group to get back together to work with him in the studio. His concert performance of the song pays homage to the group's live show, which I'm sure he got to see when they were on Capitol Records together in the late '80s. He works hard to capture their incredible energy.

Within the group world is a category that is smaller and has an even tougher time surviving in country music: the "girl" groups. There have been several outstanding groups made up entirely of women. In the mid-'80s the Forrester Sisters made a big splash in town with several hits. Suddenly, there were several all-female groups signed to major labels. Wild Rose, the McCarters and the Burch Sisters made inroads into the business, but were unable to break out early enough to stay together.

In 1998, the Dixie Chicks broke through after years of work, and have become the darlings of the music business. Last fall, they picked up the CMA's

Horizon and Vocal Group of the Year awards, something no other group has ever done in the same year.

At the 1999 *Grammy Awards*, they were honored with the awards for Best Country Album and Best Country Vocal Performance by a Duo or Group. In May of 1999, their first Monuement album, *Wide Open Spaces*, was close to selling six million copies, and received the ACM's Album of the Year award. They also matched their CMA wins by taking home the ACM awards for Best New Vocal Group or Duo and Top Vocal Group or Duo, breaking Brooks and Dunn's six-year hold on that award. Look for more girl groups on the Row, now that the Chicks have made it. Hopefully, more will survive this cycle.

Several new groups also made inroads during the '90s. The Kentucky Headhunters surprised everyone (including themselves), at the 1990 CMAs by picking up Group and Album of the Year. Diamond Rio grew out of the Tennessee River Boys, a band that performed at Opryland in the '80s. In the '90s, they picked up four CMA Group of the Year awards and many other nominations. The Mavericks picked up wide acclaim and won the CMA's Vocal Group of the Year award in 1995 and 1996, but couldn't get played on country radio. Their fabulously eclectic music has led them to seek other formats to get airplay, but they haven't left Nashville, except to go on tour. They recently left for England and Europe on a tour that has already sold 60,000 tickets, including six sold-out performances at the Royal Albert Hall in London.

Many groups have come and gone in the last few years. Other groups that did well in the '90s include Confederate Railroad, Blackhawk, Lonestar, Ricochet and BR5-49. All of them are working hard to keep it together and continue their success. Among the newest groups just bubbling to the top are Sons of the Desert, Perfect Stranger, The Great Divide, Cactus Choir and South Sixty Five.

This page: Three "Girl Groups" meet backstage at Fanfair. The first three on the left are The Burch Sisters, the next three are The McCarters, and the final four are The Forester Sisters (1989); Facing page, clockwise from top left: The Sons of the Desert showcase during Country Radio Seminar (1998); Retro-country group, BR5-49, got their name from the television program Hee-Haw (1996); Lonestar receives an award from Country Music Television (1996); The three guys on the right are the group, Blackhawk, hanging out with their band members, of the left (1994).

Recently, Nashville seems to have adopted the Canadian family group the Wilkinsons. Made up of the children, Amanda and Tyler, and father, Steve, their family harmony follows the early country music traditions that spawned groups like the Carter Family and the Stonemans. Their first Giant Records single, "26 Cents," co-written by Steve Wilkinson and William Wallace, climbed to number one in the fall of 1998, capping a whirlwind year that also included opening for Vince Gill and Alan Jackson. The year 1999 brought them three ACM nominations in both group categories and for Single of the Year. Not bad, considering that only a year ago they were unknown immigrants to Nashville. Look for them to have a great career in the twenty-first century. ▣

The Statler BROTHERS

The Statler Brothers pick up yet another Vocal Group award on the TNN Music City News Awards Show (1993).

I first heard of the Statler Brothers like most of the rest of the world. One day, in 1965, while driving somewhere in my dad's '55 Chevy, I heard "Countin' Flowers on the Walls" on the radio and loved it. I bought the single and wore it out. The lyrics were deliciously twisted for a teenage boy, and their harmonies were wonderful. Little did I know that in ten years, I'd be photographing them.

These guys honed their skills in their hometown of Staunton, Virginia, playing in churches and at local gatherings of all kinds. They were drawn together by the sound of the southern Gospel quartets, like the legendary Blackwood Brothers, and, for a while, called themselves the Kingsmen. But their interest in performing went beyond the Gospel world, and the songs they were writing addressed the secular themes found in popular and country music. Harold and Don Reid, Lew DeWitt and Phil Balsley were dreaming of taking their act on the road.

They got their big break in 1963, when Johnny Cash had the chance to hear them. It was during this time that the group changed their name to the Statler Brothers, taking the name from a box of tissues that just happened to be in the hotel room that day. Johnny soon added them to his show and introduced them to the executives at his label, Columbia Records. They recorded "Flowers on the Wall" while on a lunch break during one of the first sessions. As happens quite often in the music business, the song that was done off the cuff became the hit that brought them to national prominence, winning the 1965 Grammy for Best Pop Vocal Performance by a Duo or Group.

I had the opportunity to see them perform with Johnny Cash on his ABC television show in the early 1970s. We came down from Clarksville, Tennessee, to the Ryman Auditorium several times for the tapings, and each time, they were featured on a number. In 1972, as their fame grew, they left Johnny's show to establish a career on their own, soon picking up a second Grammy for their performance of "Class of '57."

By the time I moved to Nashville, they were on Mercury Records, being produced by the great Jerry Kennedy, who had produced Roger Miller's records in the 1960s and created the guitar lick that helped make Roy Orbison's "Oh, Pretty Woman" one of the best selling singles of that decade. Their collaboration, which started in 1970, has continued

to this day, earning Jerry the nickname the "Fifth Statler Brother."

Apparently, the collaboration worked. Soon, the Statlers were the dominant vocal group in country music. The CMA named them Vocal Group of the Year nine times between 1972 and 1984. Between 1971 and 1997, they picked up the Music City News award for Vocal Group every year except 1983, when the award went to Alabama.

In the mid-'70s, the Statlers created a fictional group whose recordings are among the funniest ever made. Lester "Roadhog" Moran and the Cadillac Cowboys came out of their memories of the local live radio shows they'd heard in their youth. First appearing on their 1972 album *Country Music...Then and Now*, Roadhog's antics became so popular that they recorded a whole album. *Alive at the Johnny Mack Brown High School* was released in 1974, and some fans, not realizing that this was a parody, were miffed at Lester's comments about the Statlers.

Lester and the gang disappeared for a number of years, and the album was forgotten. In the early '80s, someone on the Mercury Records staff noticed that the record had sold enough units to rise to the status of "plywood," for sales of 1250 or more albums. In reality, as Statler fans caught on to the joke, it had sold more than 100,000. Lester "Roadhog" Moran and the Cadillac Cowboys were coaxed out of "retirement" long enough to receive their award in a motel room somewhere on the outskirts of Nashville. Since then, they've moved back to Rainbow Valley, Virginia, where legend has it they became the best janitorial staff that Johnny Mack Brown High School ever had.

In the early 1980s, Lew Dewitt had to leave the group because of chronic health problems brought on by an intestinal condition known as Crohn's disease. A few years later, when his health was better, he produced a solo project and appeared at Fanfair once more on the Independent Label show. Sadly, though, his condition worsened again, and in 1990, the world lost a very nice man and great songwriter. It was Lew who had written "Flowers on the Wall," the song that brought the Statler Brothers to everyone's attention in 1965.

When he left the group in 1982, the three remaining guys didn't have to look very far to find someone to fill his shoes. Jimmy Fortune, also a Virginia boy, had been heard by Lew DeWitt during that time and was able to perform for them before they opened auditions in Nashville. They didn't look any further. Jimmy joined the group and made his Fanfair debut the following year. He was immediately accepted by the fans who had supported the group from the beginning. Jimmy's abilities as a songwriter also brought them one of their best songs, the heart-tugging patriotic ballad "More Than a Name on the Wall."

In 1991, the Statler Brothers started their long-

The Statlers make their mark for the Grammy Walkway of Stars (1989).

running variety show on the Nashville Network, with producer Jim Owens, who created the *Music City News Awards* several years before. For much of the '90s, it was the top-rated show on the network. Since they brought their music to Nashville, the group has recorded over thirty-five albums, with sales of more than fifteen million copies.

The Statler Brothers' influence on other groups who have made their mark since then is obvious. From the Oak Ridge Boys, who grew out of a Gospel choir in eastern Tennessee, to the Forester Sisters, who started singing in their church in Rising Fawn, Georgia, the use of the quartet sound in country music has grown. These performers' success continues to encourage record labels to gamble on vocal groups. Alabama, Sawyer Brown, Shenandoah, Lonestar, Ricochet and the other groups who have been given a chance should always be grateful to the boys from Virginia for proving that it could be done.

4 **THE GIRL SINGERS**

A Force To Be
Reckoned With

Clockwise from left: Patsy Montana is one of the Women of Country Music honored on the TV special (1992); k. d. Lang, Kitty Wells, Loretta Lynn & Brenda Lee perform on the CMA Award Show (1988); Minnie Pearl performs on the Grand Ole Opry (1988).

From the beginning, women in country music have had to work hard to gain recognition and respect. Often referred to as the girl singer in the band, a woman was looked upon as a novelty act. The songs women sang usually were aimed toward the men in the audience, and their appearance reflected this. When they toured on the road with men, rumors followed. Many people automatically presumed the worst about them. But the strong ones survived this diversion from their talent. Artists like Patsy Montana and Kitty Wells and the wonderful Minnie Pearl set high standards for the women who followed in their footsteps.

These pioneers quickly gained the respect of the men as their success continued. In 1935, when Patsy Montana's "I Wanna Be a Cowboy's Sweetheart" became the first million-selling record by a female artist, the music business realized just how marketable the ladies could be. Soon, native Nashvillian Kitty Wells joined Patsy as a successful artist with great popularity on radio and onstage, when she wasn't taking care of her children. When she heard Hank Thompson's song "Wild Side of Life," she felt the need to respond to the idea that it was the woman's fault when they compromised their virtue by hanging out in the bars. She countered the idea with "It Wasn't God Who Made Honkey Tonk Angels," and found a vast audience who agreed with what she had to say. That single eventually passed the one-million

Clockwise from top left: Sarah Cannon(aka Minnie Pearl) peeks over Roy Acuff's shoulder as he reads the names of the Horizon award nominees (1987); the Honky Tonk Angels, Loretta Lynn, Dolly Parton & Tammy Wynette, perform on the CMA Awards Show (1993); Loretta Lynn performs in her theater in Branson, Missouri (1992).

mark in sales, and continues to be popular to this day. She's been called "The Queen of Country Music" ever since.

Meanwhile, Ward-Belmont graduate Sarah Cannon created a stage character that won the hearts of the regular listeners of the Grand Ole Opry. Minnie Pearl, a single gal from Grinder's Switch who eyed the men and told stories about the folks back home, set a standard in comedy that eventually landed her not only in the Country Music Hall of Fame but in the Comedy Hall of Fame as well. Offstage, she became one of Nashville's most respected citizens. The advice and friendship she gave to women and men alike in the music business made her probably the most revered artist in country music to this day. Just ask Garth & Sandy Brooks and Amy Grant, who honored her when they named their children.

In the late '50s, Nashville's siren call brought a singer from Virginia who would add even more respect to women working in the music business. Patsy Cline's rendition of "Walkin' After Midnight" on Arthur Godfrey's show in 1957 opened a big door for her to walk through, which led her to Owen Bradley at Decca records. Her renditions of "Crazy," "I Fall to Pieces" and "Sweet Dreams" still are among the best recordings made in Nashville. She influenced many women to pursue music as a career, from Loretta Lynn to k. d. lang. Tragically, in 1963, she died in a plane crash before she could carry her career farther. In 1991, when MCA Records released a re-mastered greatest hits album, she achieved

multi-platinum sales, rivaling Garth Brooks as his career was just taking off. No one had forgotten about her. No one will.

When she died, her new friend, Loretta Lynn, was just getting started. She'd managed to jump-start a career with the support of her husband, Mooney, who believed in her at a time when most men preferred their wives stay home with the babies. Of course, she did that, too, as much as possible. She's always credited him with her making it in country music, but her writing skills and down-home country voice were what attracted radio stations to play her records. From songs like "You Ain't Woman Enough to Take My Man," which dealt with the hard part of marriage, to "One's on the Way," which addressed the everyday life of a housewife, she told the truth about what women were going through.

Lorett's signature song, "Coal Miner's Daughter," described her hard life as a child with reverence and hope. It reached those who were still struggling in a

world she was lucky enough to escape as she found her way to Nashville. Her autobiography of the same name was a major best-seller as a book and a highly acclaimed movie that garnered Sissy Spacek an Academy Award for her hauntingly authentic portrayal of Loretta in 1980. To this day, she continues to influence other women, like her sisters Crystal Gayle and Peggy, her cousin Patty Loveless and her own daughters, the Lynns, to pursue music as a career.

The early '60s brought another young lady into country music. From Georgia via the pop charts, Brenda Lee came to Nashville after major success as a teen star.

Though her songs first hit the airwaves on the rock and roll charts, many of her influences were from here. Soon, she found her way here, too, all the way to the Country Music Hall of Fame. She's become a roll model for the young ladies who've since come here in hopes of making it in the music business. From Tanya Tucker to DreamWorks new artist, Jessica Andrews, they've all listened to her advice. And, believe me, "Little Miss Dynamite" will tell you the truth.

In the late '60s and early '70s, as the door was opening for women in country music, several other careers were launched. Jeannie C. Riley caused a firestorm of controversy in 1968 with her song "Harper Valley PTA." Written by the great song-

Clockwise from top left: Katherine & Owen Bradley attend the BMI Awards Dinner (1989); Loretta Lynn & Conway Twitty surprise the audience during Fanfair week (1987); Loretta's biggest and most loyal fan, Mooney Lynn (1983); Loretta Lynn sings "You Ain't Woman Enough to Take My Man" to her husband, Mooney, on the Music City News Awards Show (1983); Loretta Lynn sings on the CMA 30th Anniversary Special (1988).

writer Tom T. Hall, it addressed the problems single mothers were facing in society and attacked the hypocrisy of passing judgment on others. She won CMA's Single of the Year in 1968, and received Female Vocalist nominations in 1968 and 1969.

The success of the song led to several Grammy nominations, including one for Song of the Year, which she lost to Simon & Garfunkle's "Mrs. Robinson." Jeannie won for Country Female Vocal Performance, beating her peers Tammy Wynette and Dottie West for the trophy. A movie and a TV series followed soon after. Other female artists bubbling up to the top at that time included Lynn Anderson, Donna Fargo and a young lady named Dolly Parton.

Dottie West brought a little "Country Sunshine"

to the charts with her award-winning hit in 1973. She was a sweet lady who helped the careers of many other stars, including Steve Wariner. Tragically, she died in 1991 in a car accident while on the way to perform on the Grand Old Opry, where she had been a member since in 1964. She is missed by all who knew her. There's a memorial highway named in her honor in her hometown of McMinnville, Tennessee.

Lynn Anderson

Lynn Anderson was born into the business. Her parents, Liz and Casey, were already successful as songwriters and publishers when their daughter began pursuing a career as a country singer. When she married Glen Sutton and moved to Nashville, the ball really started rolling. Glen Sutton, known for

Left to right: Little Miss Dynamite, Brenda Lee, performs on Nashville Now! (1984); Fifteen-year-old Tanya Tucker sings on the show In Concert (1975); Lynn Anderson sings "Under the Boardwalk" on TNN's New Country (1988); Dottie West makes a surprise visit to the Stockyard's Bullpen Lounge (1985).

great songs like "Almost Persuaded," produced her major hits including "Rose Garden." That collaboration brought them Grammys in 1971 and established her as a country star.

Dolly Parton

Dolly Parton, one of twelve children, came from Sevierville, just miles from the Smoky Mountains in eastern Tennessee. With lots of uncles and cousins around as well, this close-knit family took care of each other during the hard times. When Dolly showed an interest in music, she received encouragement from her mother, Avie Lee Parton. When you meet her mother, you see where Dolly got her courage and bright attitude. I asked her once how many children she had. She listed them, then mentioned that one

had been stillborn. "I carried him for nine months, so I still count him. He's buried up there in the family plot." I was deeply moved by her honesty and her belief in her children. Most of the other kids followed Dolly into the music business with their parent's blessings. Sisters Stella and Frieda and brother Randy sought record deals, and brother Fred wrote her number-one duet with Ricky Van Shelton, "Rockin' Years." Baby sister Rachel played her "nine-to-five" role on a short-lived TV series.

Dolly got her first big break when Porter Wagoner asked her to be on his very popular television show. Soon, their duets and her solos brought

Tammy WYNETTE

From the same part of Mississippi that gave us Elvis Presley came a young lady who loved to sing. When her first marriage fell apart, she moved to Birmingham and worked as a beautician while trying to raise her children. By the time Tammy Wynette got to Nashville, she knew what to write about and what to sing. Though many people think of her as fragile because of her recent illnesses and untimely death, I see her as an incredibly strong and gracious woman. From my first experience with her, when she was close to the divorce from George Jones, to the last time I saw her and husband, George Richey I saw only strength. She didn't want anyone to think of her problems. And when you were in her house, she was concerned about your comfort.

In 1974, my friend Diane suggested that I photograph a benefit concert for Ivory Joe Hunter, a Memphis writer, who, by the way, was black. He was suffering greatly with cancer, and his friends came together for him to help him pay his medical bills. They included Tex Ritter's widow, Issac Hayes, and George and Tammy Wynette. I was impressed.

The music was great, but it was obvious that George and Tammy were having problems. They were bouncing barbed comments at each other between songs and looked uncomfortable together. Still, they did what they could for their friend who was hurting.

Tammy Wynette performs on Nashville Now! (1986).

A few months later, they split up. Their divorce and eventual rekindled friendship is stuff of legend now. In recent years, George affectionately referred to George Richey as "husband-in-law."

My first personal encounter with her was at the house she and George Jones had lived in before the divorce. She and second George were still living there, and Epic Records was doing a video to support her upcoming single. Their house became the studio. Between takes, she kept asking the crew if they needed a Coke or something. She thought of us as guests in her house.

At one point, I wandered into the living room and looked around. She walked in and I complimented her on the decor, which included Chinese vases and Persian rugs. She thanked me and offered to show me her favorite room. She led me down the hall to a louvered door in the hallway. She opened it for me. Inside was a small chair in front of an easel. The walls were covered with kid graffiti. Then she told me why it meant so much.

"When Georgette was small, and we were having parties, I didn't want her to be at the other end of the house, so I made this her room. I was right down the hall if she needed me." That told me more about this woman than all the awards she won in her career. Over the years, my encounters with her only increased my esteem for this woman.

In August of 1995, I had the opportunity to visit her new house on Franklin Road. This time, she was hosting a birthday party for another entertainment legend who was coming to town. Mama Mae Axton asked her help in honoring her Hollywood friend, Milton Berle, a task which she graciously accepted. A guest list was soon compiled. Those attending included Crystal Gayle, Bryan White, Holly Dunn and Ray Stevens.

Like her previous home, the place was filled with beautiful furniture and interesting souvenirs. One that caught Milton's eye was the autographed lead sheet from a session Tammy had done with another superstar. The song was "A Woman's Needs" and it was signed, "Dearest Tammy. The Queen of Country meets The Queen of England!! Thanks Love You. Elton." Everyone got a big laugh out of that one. In another room was a beautiful portrait of Tammy that we all would later see on the stage at her memorial service at the Ryman in 1998.

But that night was full of fun and southern hospitality. They opened their house to us, introducing her guests to her hometown friends and giving guided tours. There was cake and champagne, and finally Milton opened a large number of presents. The biggest hit was a cowboy hat, which he immediately tried on. Seeing cigar-chomping Uncle Miltie in that hat brought laughter to the whole room. In fact, there was a lot of laughter that night with one of comedy's kings in the house. Through it all, Tammy made us all feel right at home.

I was hesitant, at first, to photograph the fur-nishings in her house, so I asked her if it was all right. She didn't mind at all—she in fact enjoyed the folks trooping through her house posing for pictures. Holly Dunn was amazed at the size of her walk-in closet and dressing room, which resembled a beauty parlor (more beautiful than the one Tammy had worked at in Birmingham many years ago). Everyone marveled at the size of their bathtub.

A few months later Tammy appeared last minute on *Music City Tonight* to debunk the story running in the *National Inquirer* that she was near death. She was robust and very talkative, concerned that her bookings would fall. She wanted to assure her friends and fans that she was doing fine. She later won a lawsuit against the magazine. Sadly though, just three years later, she passed away while taking a nap on the couch in her living room.

Tammy's funeral was something reserved only for kings and presidents. Carried live on CNN, the service allowed her fans worldwide to mourn with her family and friends in Nashville. The only other celebrity funeral I can recall broadcast like that was Sammy Davis Jr.'s, a few years before. It was riveting, with performances by Wynonna Judd and Lorrie Morgan, and wonderful stories by her peers. Though she was gone, she would not be forgotten.

Clockwise from top: Tammy Wynette & George Jones share a laugh on Music City Tonight (1995); Tammy Wynette helps Milton Berle blow out the candles on his birthday cake during a party at her house (1995); Tammy Wynette & George Jones sing together at a charity benefit shortly before their divorce (1974).

her onto the radio and record chart. In December 1970, "Joshua" became her first number-one record. Songs like "Coat of Many Colors" reflected the life she'd had, living at the poverty line in rural Appalachia. "Jolene" and "I Will Always Love You" led a streak of number ones she had through the early '70s. In 1976, she parted ways with Porter Wagoner and moved on with her solo career, with CMA Female Vocalist honors in 1975 and 1976. In 1978, she was named Entertainer of the Year. Inside country music, she was a growing star. Outside the business, she was held up to ridicule for her looks and her "country-ness." But that would not stop this determined woman in her quest for even greater stardom.

Dolly's increasing fame finally gave her a chance to appear on the *Johnny Carson Show*. She had been fodder for his joke machine for years, and finally, they would meet face-to-face. I remember watching it, thinking Johnny would destroy her. Instead, she took the bull by the horns from the moment she sat down. Before he could make any remarks, she told the first Dolly Parton joke. He was stunned. Her charm and her ability to make fun of herself soon had Johnny eating out of the palm of her hand. In the end, he was inviting her back and singing her praises. Though he may have told a few more Dolly jokes after that, she had successfully impressed millions of viewers with her savvy and her songs.

Dolly has continued to expand her horizons. Her foray into acting has landed her many roles, including the box office hits *Nine to Five* and *Fried Green Tomatoes*. Dolly's line of wigs and cosmetics are selling well, as has her autobiography. In 1987, she opened "Dollywood" in the foothills of the Smokies near the place where she grew up. Since then, sleepy Pigeon Forge has become a boomtown. Her theme park is one of the most popular in the country, eclipsing Opryland in the mid-'90s shortly before it closed.

Her park and the surrounding businesses that have sprung up employ hundreds of people who otherwise might have had to leave home to find work. This might be her biggest accomplishment to date: becoming a hometown hero. Now, if she could only help us find world peace.

Crystal Gayle

The late '70s and early '80s saw a number of female artists make an impact on this town. Loretta's little sister, Crystal Gayle, hit the airwaves singing hits like the million-selling single "Don't It Make My Brown Eyes Blue" and the beautiful Jack Clement song "When I Dream." Her honey-filled vocals garnered her CMA's female vocalist honors in 1977 and 1978. She was also one of the first country artists to play in China. Known for her floor-length hair, which flows around her like a cape as she sings, she continues to perform regularly around the world.

Barbara Mandrell

When Mary and Irby Mandrell encouraged their daughters to become entertainers, I don't think even they knew how far those girls would go. After Barbara took home the CMA Entertainer of the Year trophy twice in the early '80s, and with sisters Louise

Clockwise from left: Jeannie C. Riley signs her name on a plaque for the Nashville's Grammy Starwalk, now displayed outside the Grand Ole Opry (1989); Crystal Gayle makes her debut at Fanfair (1994); Vince Gill & Dolly Parton share a hug after debuting their duet of "I Will Always Love You" on the Grand Ole Opry (1996); Dolly Parton & Porter Wagoner share a laugh in the Ryman's old dressing rooms during the taping of her TV show (1988).

and Erlene had a hit television show, they surely knew they had done the right thing. About that time, I was working part-time for photographer Dennis Carney. He worked extensively with the Mandrells after they moved to Nashville. He also worked with Dolly and Conway a lot, so being around his studio was always fun.

After their success, the Mandrells agreed to model for a friend's trucking firm here in Nashville. They borrowed an airplane hangar so we could shoot this fully equipped big rig inside. Barbara and Louise were dressed in backless evening gowns and high heels. Though we were indoors, the hangar was freezing cold, so in between takes, they would run to one of the small offices and huddle around a space heater, drinking coffee to chase away the goosebumps.

As we were getting lights ready for one more take, Louise and Barbara were chatting in front of the truck's big chrome grille. Always the joker, Louise gently pushed her sister's bare back against the frigid chrome. Barbara let out a big scream and began chasing Louise around the truck. In those tight dresses, they were running in baby steps, with heels tapping on the cold concrete floor. It was hilarious. I later heard that while they were doing the TV show, Louise had a special cake made for Barbara's birthday. When she leaned over to blow out the candles, it exploded in her face. I'd have loved to see that.

In the late 1990's, Barbara put her musical career aside to pursue acting full-time in California. She has made a number of television appearances including a

regular role on a soap opera. But don't be surprised to see her returning to her roots from time to time.

Early '80s

A number of other women came into prominence during the early '80s. Sylvia had several hits, including "Drifter" and "Nobody," both of which made to the top of the charts. Janie Frickie took

home female vocalist honors in 1982 and 1983 after a number of years as a background vocalist and jingle singer. With several hits of her own, like "Down to My Last Broken Heart," she also had hit duets with Charlie Rich and Merle Haggard.

K. T. Oslin

For several years, Reba McEntire dominated the female vocalist categories of every award show, causing people to wonder if any other women would ever challenge her. The late '80s brought the answers, with several performers making their marks on country music. In 1988, K. T. Oslin came to prominence with "'80s Ladies," a song that touched upon the changes women had gone through since the '50s. Up against her that year was song writing legend Harlan Howard, for Ricky Van Shelton's hit "Life Turned Her That Way." As I took photos for the *CMA*

Awards program, I congratulated Harlan and wished him luck. He immediately said, "No, this one belongs to K. T." Nashville's answer to Irving Berlin thought she'd written a masterpiece. He was right.

Kathy Mattea

One of my all-time favorite people to work with is Kathy Mattea. A few years ago, after a party, she turned to me and said, "Alan, you've been taking pictures of me since before I want to remember." The first time I photographed her for Mercury Records, she had been drawn into a most unusual situation. Bob Beckham, a publisher who helped the careers of

writers like Kris Kristofferson and Larry Gatlin through his company Combine Music, decided to have the 1st Annual Horse Turd Throwing Contest at his house outside of Mt. Juliet. Kathy was "volunteered" for this event. The pictures I took that day continue to haunt her to this day.

Any artist starting out has to take whatever personal appearances that are available. Kathy had many of those, including handling rattlesnakes and almost learning to sky-dive. She was sweet and determined and a joy to work with, and her folksy West Virginia voice appealed to me. For her first single, "Street Talk," Mercury Records chose to dress her in fake leather pants, an image that didn't fit her at all. When the label changed management, they almost dropped her, but she wouldn't quit. When she hooked up with producer Alan Reynolds, her career changed for the better. Soon, Kathy found her voice in country music. Her first successful single, "Love at the Five and Dime," peaked on the *Billboard* charts in May of 1986 at number five. She followed this with several wonderful releases, including "Eighteen Wheels and a Dozen Roses," which went

on to win Single of the Year at the *CMA Awards* in 1988.

It was a pleasure photographing her that night. It was an even greater pleasure to cover her wins over the next two years as the Female Vocalist honoree. The song "Where've You Been," written by her husband, Jon Vezner, and Don Henry, picked up a Grammy and touched the heart of anyone with a heart. She continues to surprise everyone, including herself, by winning more awards, such as the 1997 Video of the Year for "455 Rocket" directed by Steve Goldman.

Kathy also took on the establishment when she made an effort on behalf of the victims of AIDS, after a friend of hers died from the disease. She wanted to get people to wear red ribbons in remembrance, and ran into resistance. Other people wanted to display green ribbons on behalf of the environment. In the end, the *CMA Awards* audience had some very colorful lapels in the audience, with many people wearing both ribbons. In 1995, she helped in the creation of a wonderful album and TV special, Red, *Hot and Country*, which raised funds and awareness for AIDS research. Those involved with that project were a tes-

Left to right: Kathy Mattea competes in the Bob Beckham Horse Turd Throwing Contest (1984); during Kathy Mattea's 1st Opry appearance, after being praised by Jim Ed Brown, she reveals his TNN Talent show turned her down a few years before (1988).

tament to her strength and popularity. From Carl Perkins to Billy Ray Cyrus, Earl Scruggs to Levon Helm of the Band, artists were more than ready to join her cause.

Patty Loveless

During this time, a distant cousin of Loretta Lynn's family was trying to get her foot in the door. She had come from North Carolina with her brother, Roger Ramey, to seek a musical career. I met Roger shortly after I moved to Nashville. Though he and Patty earlier had been a duo, Roger was now trying to help her become the singer in the family. She soon found a fol-

lowing of supporters despite her shyness. She got a writer's deal at the legendary Acuff-Rose Publishing Company, and, soon, she was signed by MCA Records. Her first single, "If My Heart Had Windows," made it to number ten in the *Billboard* charts in early 1988.

Patty was an immediate favorite within the industry, and was asked to join the Opry that same year. She accepted, of course. On induction night, as Porter Wagoner welcomed her to the stage, you could tell she was overjoyed.

In 1994, she touched our hearts with "How Can I Help You Say Goodbye" and, finally, won CMA's Female Vocalist of the Year in 1996.

Pam Tillis

As the daughter of country star Mel Tillis, Pam Tillis grew up around the music business. She knew firsthand what the job could do to someone's personal life when she decided to pursue the life of a performer, but it was in her blood. Her father had been involved in the business as a writer and performer since the '50s and was CMA's Entertainer in 1976, about the time she began playing in local clubs. I first remember hearing her perform rock music, though her voice had a country twang she couldn't hide. Eventually, she gave in to her roots, which soon landed her a deal at Warner Brothers Records. Though

the album she released on that label went nowhere, two cuts, "Maybe It Was Memphis" and "One of Those Things" were major hits when recut for her second label, Arista.

A little irony came with the first song Arista released in 1991. "Don't Tell Me What To Do" was written by Harlan Howard, who had penned her father's first breakthrough single, "Life Turned Her That Way," which hit the charts when Pam was ten years old.

She married another successful songwriter, Bob DePiero, in 1991, and together, they had a hit with "Cleopatra, Queen of Denial." Sadly, their marriage went sour a few years later. Still, at an award ceremony shortly after their divorce, he included her among the "thank-yous" in his acceptance speech.

Mary Chapin Carpenter

Mary Chapin Carpenter came to Nashville after being the toast of the music scene in the Washington, D.C., area. She had won almost every Wammie for which she'd been nominated by the Washington Area Music Association for a number of years. When she signed with Columbia Records, she brought this town fresh material with a different perspective. Though it took a couple of albums to get the fans' attention, her first appearance on the *CMA Awards* won her a rousing ovation. When she sang "You Don't Know Me,

Emmylou HARRIS

This page: Emmylou Harris records her Grammy award-winning album, Live at The Ryman (1991); facing page, clockwise from top: Emmylou Harris opens for Willie Nelson with Rodney Crowell on guitar to her left (1978); Emmylou Harris sits on Harlan Howard's lap after the BMI Awards Dinner (1990); the "Trio," Linda Ronstadt, Emmylou Harris & Dolly Parton join their glorious voices on the CMA Awards Show (1986); Emmylou Harris puts her bootprint on her Grammy Starwalk plaque (1993).

One of the most intriguing and original artists of the '70s came to Nashville from California after beginning her career working with Gram Parsons of the Byrds. At a time when there was a rift in the music business over politics and lifestyles, Emmylou Harris's "hippie" appearance made some members of Nashville's establishment uncomfortable, until they heard her sing. "If I Could Only Win Your Love" became her first hit, in 1975, and she quickly found herself opening for Willie Nelson. Aside from her vocal abilities, she is well known for putting together the most talented bands since Bill Monroe. Among the people she has employed over the years are Rodney Crowell, Ricky Scaggs, the Whites, Vince Gill and producers Tony Brown and Emory Gordy Jr. Her band, the Nash Ramblers, won a Grammy with her in 1992 for their album recorded at the Ryman. In 1986, she teamed up with Dolly Parton and Linda Ronstadt for one of the most glorious recordings I've ever heard. The album, *Trio*, brought many honors to them, including a CMA award, an ACM award and a Grammy. The first year I photographed the *CMA Awards*, they performed just twenty-five feet away from my front-row seat, and I was in heaven. In 1999, they released a long-awaited second album that has resulted in rave reviews and rumors of a tour.

This page: Mary Chapin Carpenter entertains on Sony Records show during Fanfair (1992); Facing page: Trisha Yearwood works on the video for "Wrong Side of Memphis" at the Ryman Auditorium (1992).

I'm the Opening Act," she connected with other artists who'd been where she was. They loved her. After that, they knew who she was.

Still, she was having a hard time connecting with some segments of the music business. At a closed industry showcase, I was irritated by two cowboys in the front row who didn't seem impressed. They sat there with their arms crossed as she sang. Everyone else seemed to be having fun. Finally, she found a song they liked. You could see it rise up through them: First, they tapped their boots, and soon, their whole bodies were

moving. When she jumped off the stage and began dancing around, they were on their feet dancing, too. "Down at the Twist and Shout" had won them over. For the rest of the set, she owned them. Radio agreed, and the song went to number two on the *Billboard* charts. It was nominated for Song of the Year in 1992, the same year she won her first Female Vocalist trophy.

Trisha Yearwood

When I photograph artists, I try to treat everyone the same; still, I have to admit, I do have my favorites.

In the summer of 1991, I went to Douglas Corner to see Pat Alger and his Algerian Trio. Kathy Mattea had just given him his first number one with "She Came From Ft. Worth" in 1990, and he'd had a hit by Garth Brooks with "Unanswered Prayers" as the year began. After he'd done a number of songs, he invited his backup vocalist to solo on a new song Garth would soon release. Trisha Yearwood's interpretation of the song, complete with the controversial third verse, absolutely stunned me. She left the audience wanting more. I made a mental note to watch this girl.

I didn't have to wait long. As 1991 started, I was asked to go to the Sound Emporium to photograph Trisha and the MCA executives who were coming over to hear some of her completed tracks. Her producer, Garth Fundis, played five songs. Label head Tony Brown was impressed and asked his staff to put together a budget for a video of what would become her first release. That following June, the song "She's in Love with the Boy," penned by John Ims, went number one as she performed at her first Fanfair. That fall, she opened for Garth Brooks on the road and has been on a roll ever since.

In 1994, I had the honor of photographing Trisha's marriage to Robert Reynolds of the Mavericks. I'd seen this budding romance growing for a while, and when they asked me, I was thrilled. They had chosen the Ryman for their chapel, an event

that would become the first in the newly restored Mother Church of Country Music. Trisha and Robert are very proud of that distinction.

The years 1997 and 1998 brought her back-to-back CMA Female Vocalist awards, a Grammy and an Oscar-nominated song from the movie *Conair*. In 1998, she sang with Pavarotti in Italy for one of his charities, opening her up to a whole new audience. In 1999, she had a guest role on the TV series *Jag*. As of this writing, the fall 1999 will see the release of a long-awaited duet album with Garth.

1999 started off well for Trisha. She was asked to join the Grand Ole Opry during a special show at the Ryman, on the same spot where Hank & Patsy used to sing, and where she and Robert were married.

Following her heroes into that venerated family, knowing that she will help carry their memories into the next century, has got to be the thrill of a lifetime. I know, from talking to them that night, that the Opry folks are just as thrilled to have her in the fold.

On March 13, Trisha became the seventy-first member of the Opry. In the program for that night, there's a quote from Porter Wagoner that says it all: "I have always been one of Trisha's biggest fans, and I know how important it is to her to become part of the Opry family. And as part of that family myself, I am very excited to welcome such a talented, beautiful and kind woman. The lights in the Opry will shine a little brighter from now on."

Alison Krauss

In 1986, I was called by someone with Kentucky Fried Chicken to go cover a session with their latest contest winner. Sam Bush, the creator of New Grass Revival, was to be the producer, so I knew we'd have a

good time, no matter who the winner was. I expected a session where Sam would be able to doctor it up, despite the artists' inexperience. Boy, was I wrong!

In came a teenage fiddle player and her band, young and wide-eyed over this chance. When they started playing and she put her fiddle down long enough to sing, I was impressed. This young bluegrasser knew what she was doing. It was obvious that she was going somewhere. Soon after, she had a deal with Rounder Records. Alison Krauss and her band Union Station had made a really good start.

By the mid-'90s, they'd become well-known among the bluegrass circles, even winning Grammys for their albums, but most people still hadn't heard her. Inside the music business in Nashville, she was impressing her peers, recording with Vince and Dolly and making several important TV appearances. Slowly, her talents were being recognized. At the age of 21, in 1993, she was inducted into the Opry . Then, in 1994, RCA Records asked her to be part of a tribute album to Keith Whitley. She accepted.

I was asked to go by the session early in the afternoon, shortly before another job. When I got there, Alison was working hard to perfect one of the fiddle portions of the song. They kept playing the track over and over, so I sat down to listen. At one point, when she came in to listen, she apologized for taking so long. I said, "As long I get to hear you sing, I'm fine." I had to leave and come back to get the photos, but what I heard was worth it.

"When You Say Nothing at All" became her breakthrough into the country charts and beyond. The song was also included on a "best hits" release on Rounder Records. That album went on to sell more than any bluegrass album in history. It was nominated for Album of the Year by the CMA, until they realized it was a compilation album and therefore not qualified for the category. The CMA voters were so enamored of this new discovery that they wanted to nominate her for everything.

In 1995, the CMA gave her the Horizon Award, Single of the Year, Female Vocalist and Vocal Event Award with Shenandoah for "Somewhere in the Vicinity of the Heart." Backstage in the press room, she seemed stunned as, over and over again, she came back for an interview. Today, you can hear her on radio stations in many formats: bluegrass, country and Americana. She was one of the artists asked to participate in DreamWorks *The Prince of Egypt* Nashville album project. Her cut "I Give to You His Heart" is one of the most popular.

Jo Dee Messina

A few years ago, at a Curb Records luncheon, Tim McGraw introduced us to this little spunky redhead from Massachusetts, not a place one could think would produce a budding country star. But country music knows no boundaries, and neither does Jo Dee Messina. You could see the hopeful spark in her eye that day as she sang to tracks, trying to get our attention. More than her singing that day, I was struck by

This page: Horizon award nominee Jo Dee Messina performs on the CMA Awards Show (1998); Facing page: Alison Krauss & Union Station record "When You Say Nothing at All" with Randy Scruggs, 2nd from the right, producing (1994);

The JUDDS

My first encounter with Naomi Judd was when I was working for photographer Dennis Carney in the early 1980's. At the time she was a single mother working as a nurse and modeling when she could. She had come out with her boyfriend, Larry Strickland, and his band, Memphis, to help them with their makeup during a publicity session. She was charming and positive, and soon became one of our favorite visitors. Even when she wasn't working on a job there, she would stop by to say hello and have a cup of coffee. More than once, she brought her teenage daughter, Wynonna, with her. We finally met her younger daughter, Ashley, when she came to one of our Christmas parties, impressing us with her poise and beauty. We didn't know they were going to be famous, we just liked them.

Naomi was very quiet about their interest in the music business, preferring to concentrate on her modeling when she visited us. She never dwelled on how broke they were or on the hardships they were enduring that time. A year or so after I left there, I heard a new song on the radio, and after it was over, the announcer said, "That was 'Had a Dream', by the new duo, The Judds." "I wonder if they're kin to Naomi?", I thought to myself. I soon found out.

Backstage at the 1984 Music City News Awards there were Naomi and Wynonna, meeting the stars that had inspired them. The dream that they'd had for years was just beginning. "Mama, He's Crazy", their second single, had gone to number one in Billboard just a week before the show, and everyone backstage wanted to meet them, as well.

That fall, the CMA gave them the Horizon Award, fully believing that they were here to stay. "Mama, He's Crazy" would soon bring them the 1984 Grammy for Best Country Performance by a Duo or Group, followed the next year by the same award for "Why Not Me?". Eventually, they would take home three more. Throughout their existence they were nominated for twenty CMA Awards, taking home nine of the trophies. The Music City News Awards gave them every vocal duo award from 1985

This page: The Judds receive their last CMA Vocal Group of the Year award before announcing their retirement (1991); facing page: The Judds perform at their finale concert in Murfreesboro, Tennessee (1992).

This page: Wynonna, Naomi and Ashley Judd wait backstage before the CMA Awards Show (1993); facing page: Wynonna introduces her first child, Elijah, to her fanclub (1995).

through 1992. The Academy of Country Music honored them as Vocal Duet seven years in a row. Meanwhile, Ashley was in college at the University of Kentucky studying literature and dreaming of acting someday.

With the help of producer Brent Maher and guitarist, and mentor, Don Potter, they had been able to share their magic sound with the rest of the world. Starting out a little bit shy, they soon blossomed into great entertainers. They always had the most talented musicians available, and soon learned how to work the stage with the best of them. But the family harmonies, honed around the kitchen table during the lean times as Naomi raised her children, were their biggest selling point. It wasn't long before they were a household name.

Sadly, all of this came to an end after Naomi contracted Hepatitis-C, a deadly blood disease, probably from her days as a nurse. At the 1989 CMA Awards Show, they were unusually somber and emotional as they accepted their Vocal Duo award. Though they knew Naomi's health was going to force her to retire, they didn't want to spoil the

awards show for everyone else. A few weeks later, they dropped the bombshell at a tearful press conference, and announced they would fulfill their concert obligations on what would become their farewell tour. The final show was held in Murfreesboro, Tennessee, on December 4th, 1991.

A month before the show, I was at the concert venue, The Murphy Center, to cover Garth Brooks' concert, when I noticed a line of people winding around the corner. Thinking they were there early for Garth's show, I stopped to talk to some of them. "Oh, no, we're here for The Judds tickets that go on sale tomorrow," one young lady told me after I ask if they were excited to see Garth. The next day, the tickets sold out in no time.

The day of the concert, I arrived early in the afternoon to photograph setup and some of the rehearsal. The girls were understandably emotional,

going though tissues like crazy as they stopped to wipe away the tears. Everyone was in a somber mood as they tried to prepare for the show for the last time. Naomi knew how she was going to be during the show, so she stashed a box of Kleenex and a small makeup kit just out of sight under one of the risers. From time to time between songs, she would go over there to check her makeup and grab some new tissues. Quite often, I would see Wynonna look up in a effort to stop the tears from rolling down her cheeks. It was no different in the audience.

People had come from all over the country to be with their girls on that final night.

Many other artists like Reba McEntire, Billy Dean and Larry Gatlin were there to see it, as well. All of their friends and family were there to support them on this difficult night. Though emotions ran high, Naomi and Wynonna put on one of the best concerts I've ever seen. The Jordanaires were there to back them on a few numbers and on the final song, "Love Can Build a Bridge", the Christ Church Choir joined them on stage. I honestly expected them to ascend into the heavens as they walked up to the highest platform on the stage. As they left the stage and walked into the darkness, I saw them stop and hug each other. When the hug was over, so were The Judds.

Wynonna has gone on to have a great solo career, with five nominations on her own from the CMA and the ACM's Female Vocalist award in 1993. Ashley Judd has become a bona fide movie star with many of her performances receiving critical acclaim. As her health improved, Naomi wrote their autobiography, which immediately became a best seller and a hit made-for-TV movie. In 1995, she embarked on a career as a motivational speaker, charming her audiences with her wit and wisdom. She has since written a cookbook and, more recently, a children's book called Love Can Build a Bridge. She even has her own talk show.

After much speculation over whether The Judds would ever sing again, it would be revealed that they would reunite for one show on New Year's Eve 1999, the end of the millennium, in Phoenix, Arizona. Needless to say, tickets sold out immediately, as their loyal fans, affectionately known as "Juddheads", lined up, once again to see their girls.

As for a future tour? Only time will tell.

This page: Jo Dee Messina works on her album "I'm Alright" with producers Tim McGraw & Byron Gallimore (1997). Facing page: Leann Rimes sings Patsy Montana's signature song, "I Wanna Be A Cowboy's Sweetheart," on the CMA Awards Show (1996).

her determination and her blazing red hair. She reminded me of an Oklahoma girl I'd met many years ago named Reba McEntire.

Her first couple of singles, "Heads Carolina, Tails California" and "You're Not in Kansas Anymore," did very well, but her third single failed to follow their lead. She came close to going broke while the label delayed recording her second album. That delay, however, was a blessing in disguise, because it allowed her and her producers more time to seek out the best songs available. When she finally went into the studio with producers Tim McGraw and Byron Gallimore, she put everything she had into the music.

Their hard work paid off with *I'm Alright*, an album that has, so far, produced three back-to-back number-one singles, two of which made it into the top twenty most played songs in 1998, according to *Radio & Record* magazine. It was nominated by the Academy of Country Music for Album of the Year, up against

the Dixie Chicks, Faith Hill, Garth Brooks and George Strait. Though it didn't win, it certainly helped her capture the award for Best New Female Vocalist.

Jo Dee was truly overcome with emotion as she accepted the trophy. Choking back tears, she said, "Some roads seem long, and this one was paved with a lot of prayers, some tears and a lot of laughter." Then she thanked everyone ending with "...I pray that you will realize how much your support means to me." Believe me when I say that for anyone with the character, charm and talent that Jo Dee has, that support is easy to give. As for her future in the music business, I have a feeling "everything's gonna be alright."

Leann Rimes

When Leann Rimes showed up in Nashville a few years ago, a lot of people rolled their eyes at the idea of another teenage girl making it in country music. Though many had tried, not since Tanya Tucker burst on the scene in the '70s had any succeeded. But Mike Curb, who'd found stardom in his teens with the Mike Curb Congregation, saw how talented she was and decided to take a chance despite her age. Boy, did he make the right decision.

In 1996, the little girl blew us all away with her first single, "Blue," reminding the veterans of the days of Patsy Cline. At the same time, she was attracting a very young audience who immediately identified with her as one of them. Years of beauty pageants and talent shows gave her the poise and confidence some performers

don't achieve till years into their careers. Artists like Alan Jackson and Vince Gill scrambled to have her as an opening act, and her reception at Fanfair was exceptional for a first-year performer.

That fall, she wowed them on the *CMA Awards*, and ended the year with her first number-one song, "One Way Ticket," written by veteran songwriter Keith Hinton and 1980s MTM artist Judy Rodman. Both were pleasantly surprised by the success of the song.

Nineteen ninety-seven brought her a ton of awards. As in her early talent contest days, she was raking them

in. Grammys, ACMs, TNN/MCNs and CMAs came her way. She has since defied the odds by crossing over into the pop world, having several hits on the adult contemporary and gospel charts as well as, the country charts. It'll be interesting to see where this young lady's career will take her. As it is, her success has opened the doors for several other "underage" performers, like Lila McCann, Jessica Andrews, Alisa Elliot and the Wilkinsons' Amanda and Tyler (along with daddy Steve). Time will tell where their careers will go, but like Leann, they've gotten an early start.

Shania Twain

Canada has given country music many stars. From the 1950s, when Hall of Famer Hank Snow joined the Opry, to Anne Murray's great success in the '70s and '80s, Canada has loaned Nashville some of its most talented performers. In the '90s, performers like Michelle Wright, Terri Clark, Paul Brandt, Lisa Brokop and the Wilkinsons made strong showings south of the Canadian border. But no one expected that a young lady from Windsor, Ontario, would break every record in the book. On the 1999 Academy of Country Music Awards, Shania Twain was presented with a new RIAA sales award called the Diamond Award, which was created for sales in excess of ten million copies of one album. That night, she received two of them, for her albums *The Woman In Me* and *Come On Over*.

Shania waited until she had a few hits before touring, so she would have enough material to put on a good show. Critics panned this move, suggesting she

was just a product of her husband's studio genius. ("Mutt" Lange, known for his work with rock artists like Foreigner and Def Leppard, had spoken to her several times on the phone before meeting her at Fanfair in 1993. It wasn't long before they were an item, both personally and professionally, and in December of that year, they had been married.)

Shania and Mutt took their time writing songs and crafting her next album, trying to create a unique sound that better expressed her personality. Their patience paid off. Their first single, "Whose Bed Have Your Boots Been Under," only rose to number eleven in *Billboard* but eventually sold a million copies, certifying it as gold. The next single, "Any Man of Mine," rose to the top of all the country charts in time for her 1995 appearance on Fanfair's *Mercury* show. Her album, *The Woman In Me*, went gold in Canada and the US just in time for a Fanfair presentation. By a month later the album had gone platinum, and by the end of 1995, over four million albums had been sold.

Her second album, *Come On Over*, wasn't released until 1997, but Shania hadn't waned. Despite not touring, the singles from her previous album were well received and her momentum was growing, with award nominations and special appearances. Even her videos were selling platinum.

Finally, she had enough material and money to put together the show she wanted, and her much-awaited tour was ready to hit the road. Many of the nay-sayers expected her to fall flat on her face, but they didn't know how hard she'd worked entertaining gamblers in

This page: Shania Twain makes her 3rd Fanfair appearance as a superstar (1996). Facing page: Shania Twain makes her debut on the Mercury Records Fanfair show (1993).

the casinos of northern Canada. All of the dates sold out immediately, and the reporters who covered the opening night in her hometown sent out glowing reports of the concert.

At the *Grammy Awards* in 1999, Shania took home the statuette for Best Female Country Vocal Performance and shared the Country Song win for "You're Still The One" with her writing partner and life partner, Robert John "Mutt" Lange. A few months later, the Academy of Country Music Awards presented her with a new RIAA certification, the Diamond award, signifying sales of over ten million units of one album, for *The Woman in Me* and *Come On Over*. No other woman—and only one man, Garth Brooks—has done that in country music history.

She's also broken more ground by crossing over in a big way onto the Adult Contemporary charts, finishing 1998 with two number-one hits. "You're Still the One" finished second on R & R's AC chart for 1998 airplay, beating out heavyweights like Celine Dion, Eric Clapton and the Backstreet Boys. As she resumes touring in 1999, Shania is considered an established star. No one wonders anymore if she really has talent: now they just wonder how far her career will go as we move into the next millennium.

Faith Hill

When Michael Kosser was finishing his book, Hot Country Women, for which I was supplying the photos, we discussed who might be hot by the time it was released. I suggested a Mississippi girl named

This page: Producer Scott Hendricks and Faith Hill hold a plaque honoring the #1 single, "Wild One" (1994); facing page: Faith Hill and Lisa Stewart go after a loose ball in the Vince Gill Basketball Tournament at Belmont University (1993).

Faith Hill. I'd already met her and knew the enthusiasm of those who'd signed her at Warner Brothers Records and BMI. Martha Sharp, the same person who'd encouraged Randy Travis' signing, had faith in Faith's potential. She was right. Her first single, "Wild One," went to number one in the Billboard charts and stayed there for an unprecedented four weeks.

Since then, she's continued to climb up the rungs of this musical ladder at breakneck speed. Somewhere along the way she crossed paths with a fellow singer named Tim McGraw, fell in love and celebrated that love by recording a song with him. I've heard them sing it several times, and each time I can see their eyes grow moist. After a day of hiding their wedding from the folks attending Tim's "Swampstock" charity softball game in Start,

Louisiana, he dedicated the next song to his new bride from Starr, Mississippi, Faith Hill. "It's Your Love" went on to win Vocal Event of the Year at the CMAs in 1997, and solidified their careers and their lives. Two children and many awards later, they're still the mushiest couple in country music.

The 1999 Academy of Country Music voters nominated Faith for six awards. She took four of them home, including another Vocal Event award for her and her husband, Tim McGraw. Nobody was surprised, including previous winner, Trisha Yearwood, who told Dick Clark backstage that Faith was her pick, as well. She was especially ecstatic with the single win for "This Kiss," thanking the writers and exclaiming that the song changed her life. As if she hasn't had enough good changes, lately. Her hero and friend, Tammy Wynette, would've been very proud of the Mississippi girl's wins, considering they came on the birthday she shares with Tim and Faith's little girl, Gracie.

Her album Faith was certified triple platinum in May 1999, and in June, Faith continued her awards sweep with four TNN/Music City News Awards including Female Vocalist and the Vocal Collaboration Award with Tim for "Just To Hear You Say That You Love Me." She may complete her triple crown later in the year by winning the CMA's Female Vocalist of the Year award for 1999. With her husband's good chances to win in several categories, it won't be long before they have to give up their trophy case and build a trophy room instead. ◾

Reba McENTIRE

When Reba's mom sought advice from legend Mama Mae Axton about how to get her teenage kids into the music business, she was told to let them finish their education first. Following that advice probably made a difference in her children's lives, especially for Reba, who learned how to learn. In twenty years, she grew from a simple country girl into an elegant lady. At Mama Mae's funeral, Reba thanked her for the good advice.

I was fortunate to meet her in 1977 just after she signed her deal with Mercury Records. Producer and label head Jerry Kennedy paired her with Jacky Ward for a duet called "Three Sheets in the Wind," hoping his earlier pop success would give her a foot in the door. Later that day, she made some of her first calls to radio programmers. "What do I Do?" she asked. "Just call them and introduce yourself," she was advised. And that's just what she did. Though she'd graduated from college, her education was just beginning. I have had the privilege of following her career since then, and always look forward to the next time I work with her.

Reba came to Nashville when Music Row still seemed like a small town. The record labels were working out of converted houses and simple office buildings. Mercury Records was in the second story of a relatively new building, with Sound Stage Studios downstairs. At the time, The Statler Brothers and Tom T. Hall were the major successes on that

Reba McEntire performs on the CMA Awards Show (1989).

label, while Dolly Parton, Loretta Lynn and Barbara Mandrell were among the few women on the country charts in a business dominated by men. The young lady who used to help her father with the bulls knew she had her work cut out for her. It was obvious from the beginning that she was determined to make it.

Soon, I would have a chance to watch Reba perform for her first Fanfair audience. She stood solidly on that stage, using her God-given vocal abilities and her family's strength and support to win over new fans. Still, her radio success was slow in coming. It wasn't till the early '80s that they began to heed her early calls by making songs like "I Don't Think Love Ought To Be That Way" and "Up to Heaven" major chart successes. When she moved to MCA records in 1983, her career took off.

With the new label came a new producer. Jimmy Bowen, who'd had much success in California with artists like Frank Sinatra and Dean Martin, now was becoming a dominant force in Nashville. He brought with him a desire for the new technology he'd seen developing in studios out there. Reba would be one of the first to have the advantage of these new recording techniques, giving her a chance to learn more about her chosen career. Her first album on her new label was a major success.

Finally, in 1984, the admiration she'd gained inside the music industry and the success she was having with the public gave her the star recognition she'd deserved. That year, the CMA gave her the award for

Female Vocalist, something they would repeat for four years in a row. In 1986, they gave her the coveted Entertainer of the Year award, which has only been received by three other women: Dolly, Loretta and Barbara. That same year, she established her publishing company, which would become the nucleus of her entertainment empire, Starstruck Entertainment.

The evolution of music videos gave Reba a chance to explore acting. Her videos for "Whoever's in New England" and "Sunday Kind of Love" made her more than just a voice on the radio. She quickly learned how to use her acting talents as a vehicle for her songs on video, and in her concert appearances as well. In a few years, her abilities would translate into an acting career that continues to grow. Her TV movie *Is There Life Out There*, built around her hit of the same name, brought her rave reviews. She had a private showing of the movie for the folks in Nashville shortly before the TV premiere. The writers of the song, Susan Longacre and Rick Giles, were blown away by what she did with their idea. Reba has since filled several other movie roles, including that of another red-headed legend, Annie Oakley.

Throughout her rise to stardom, though, she's always stayed close to her family. When Reba was a child her mother encouraged the children to sing, and her father taught them about hard work. With her siblings, Alice, Pake and Susie, she learned the enjoyment of singing for audiences. While she rodeoed she got the chance to sing "The Star Spangled Banner" on occasion, something that eventually opened the doors to Nashville. In the meantime, she went to college, just like Mae Axton suggested, studying to be a teacher.

Though her first marriage to rancher Charlie Battle dissolved because their careers led them in different directions, her marriage to Narvel Blackstock put them on a course as business partners as well as husband and wife. They both saw the need for her show to become more spectacular in order to play to larger audiences. She'd experimented with lights and staging to add drama to her shows, like she did in the video for "The Last One To Know." Ticket sales began to rise to match her record sales. She entered the '90s as the preeminent female country vocalist in the business—and bigger than most of the men too. She was now setting the standards by which newer artists would be judged as they sought their way to stardom.

The early '90s brought her the highest high and the lowest low of her life. The high came with the birth of her son, Shelby, in February 1990. The low came just one year later when her road manager and most of her band were killed in a plane crash in California. She and Narvel—and, I must say, the whole industry—were devastated by that accident. I spoke to Merle Kilgore, Hank Jr.'s manager, the day of the crash before an NSAI dinner. He told me that something like this was his biggest fear. The mood that night was somber, and a moment of silence was observed in their memory.

Reba reacted with one of the most emotional albums I've ever heard. *For My Broken Heart* reflected the depths of her sorrow and touched the hearts of her fans. "Is There Life Out There," "The Greatest Man I Never Knew" and the title song were truly moving. I remember someone suggesting that MCA Records should supply hankies with every CD.

After a few months, Reba went back on the road with a new band and a greater sense of the responsibility that comes with stardom. Now, rather than trust strangers with their flying schedules, she and Narvel started their own air charter service.

Among the performers she found to work with her this time were Linda Davis and her husband, Lang. Within a couple of years, she was so impressed with Linda's talents that she tapped her for a duet rather than seek out a better-known partner. This gamble paid off for both of them, with the single and video of "Does He Love You" making it to number one on all of the charts and eventually winning a CMA award, an MCN award and a Grammy for their vocal collaboration. Linda continued to tour with Reba for a number of years until her deal with DreamWorks in 1998 pulled her away to her own career. But they remain best of friends.

Reba and Narvel soon gave Starstruck a new building and studio from which to work. Her publishing company was paying off, with writers like

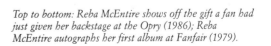

Top to bottom: Reba McEntire shows off the gift a fan had just given her backstage at the Opry (1986); Reba McEntire autographs her first album at Fanfair (1979).

Reba McEntire shows us her budding acting talents in the video for Sunday Kind of Love (1988).

Mark D. Sanders, Liz Hengber and Sunny Russ having several number ones with Reba and other artists. They also started a management and publicity company, with artists like Billy Dean and Jo Dee Messina on their roster, but Reba's touring and movie work were taking up more and more of their time, and their son, Shelby, was now of school age. After a few years, she and her husband decided to get out of handling other acts to concentrate on Reba's career. But they wisely kept the publishing company, which celebrated another number one with her song "Forever Love," the name of her latest TV movie, which also did very well.

A late '90s tour with Brooks and Dunn has been a major success, and their "triet" "If You See Him/ If You See Her" went to number one on radio and was nominated for Vocal Event of the Year in 1998. Reba went to Australia and Europe and was greeted by enthusiastic audiences who had waited years to see her in person.

So, the little country girl who went from rodeo to radio keeps racing up the charts and flying around the world like she used to ride around barrels in the arena. The reality of her long and successful career has gone well beyond her early dreams. Thanks to an education that didn't stop at the school door, Reba McEntire has truly made a mark in the world of music and made her parents extremely proud. Look for her to be around for a long, long time.

5 THE MEN

When I started trying to remember how many artists I had photographed since coming to Nashville, I was overwhelmed by how many male vocalists there had been. I quit counting at around 150. And these were performers who, at some point in the last 25 years, had a record deal with a major label. It's astonishing how many have fallen by the wayside.

In 1974, as today, certain performers dominated the charts. Marty Robbins and Porter Wagoner had syndicated television shows that were doing very well. Opry veterans like Bill Anderson and Hank Snow were still having number-one records on the radio. Conway Twitty, Merle Haggard, George Jones, Charley Pride, Tom T. Hall and Sonny James were having consistent success, while newcomers like Johnny Rodriguez and Ronnie Milsap had just had their first hits.

Glen Campbell was on a roll after becoming a household word with his influential television show, *The Glen Campbell Goodtime Hour*. Don Williams, Charlie Rich and Bobby Bare were tapping the inkwells of some of country's best songwriters with songs like "Amanda," "Behind Closed Doors" and "Marie Laveau," respectively. Willie and Waylon didn't know that they were just about to change the direction of country music. Meanwhile, George Strait had just left the army, seventeen-year-old Vince Gill had begun to perform professionally, Garth Brooks was twelve years old and Bryan White was born in February. The groundwork for Garth and Bryan's success was already being laid; they grew up hearing the music these men were making.

Merle Haggard

One of the most influential artists still performing today has got to be Merle Haggard. His abilities as a songwriter, vocalist and guitar player have influenced generations of other performers. He has been an inspiration to his peers, including Willie Nelson and Johnny Paycheck, as well as youngsters like Steve Wariner and Lee Roy Parnell. Eleven of his albums have been nominated for awards by the membership of the CMA, with two taking home trophies. At a concert at the Ryman in 1994, Merle showed the audience how that was possible. Where other artists might have run out of material, Merle kept going. At a point where it seemed he might be winding down, I went backstage for the setup shots we were supposed to do. Merle kept playing and playing. He put the Energizer bunny to shame. After another thirty minutes, someone said, "By my count, he's just done forty-two songs, and all of them were hits."

An outlaw long before Willie and Waylon, he spent time in jail and later was pardoned by Governor Ronald Reagan. His first hits, like "The Fugitive," "Branded Man" and the classic, "Mama Tried" addressed that part of his life. His songs "Workin'

Merle Haggard responds to questions after his induction into the Country Music Hall of Fame (1994).

Man Blues" and "I Take a Lot of Pride in What I Am" identified him as one of the workers. The political divide caused by the war in Vietnam soon changed his role to patriot with "Okie from Muskogee" and "The Fightin' Side of Me." His song "If We Make It Through December" is rivaled only by Dolly

Parton's "Hard Candy Christmas" as the saddest Christmas song ever written. All of these elements are fused into the one and only: Merle Haggard.

My first chance to photograph him didn't come until his son, Marty Haggard, secured a deal with MTM Records in 1985. Hoping to help his son gain some publicity, Merle stopped by the contract signing. He kept watching what I was doing, which made me nervous until I realized he simply wanted to make sure he was doing what was needed. Since then, my encounters with the "Hag" have been much less intimidating.

In 1994, many of the new artists got together to honor Merle with a tribute album called *Mama's Hungry Eyes*, which raised funds for Second Harvest Food Bank. Shortly after his induction into the Country Music Hall of Fame, Arista Records and the other participants released the project with great fanfare.

The night of the kickoff concert at the Wildhorse Saloon, Merle was on hand as the honoree. During the press conference, a reporter asked him if he was going to join the other performers that night. "Sure, why not," he said. After all, he did know the songs. The artists who were able to participate were elated. On stage were Diamond Rio, Lee Roy Parnell, Radney Foster and Steve Wariner. Joining them as the evening progressed were Lynn Anderson, Bonnie Owens, Jeff Cook of Alabama and the Father of Bluegrass, Bill Monroe.

Backstage, Frank Mull, Merle's longtime friend and sometime road manager, told me that those performers had no idea how much this evening meant to Merle. I knew what it meant to them. When the show was over, several of the artists asked me to photograph them with him. After they all were accommodated, I asked Steve Wariner to take my picture with Merle and Bill Monroe. (Thanks, Steve, you did a great job.)

Bobby Bare

I first became aware of Bobby Bare during the "Hootenanny" days of the '60s, when we would hold sing-alongs during junior-high assemblies. Two of the songs, "500 Miles Away from Home" and "Four Strong Winds," were his. When I heard him sing them, he made me feel the sadness. He was the first of my musical heroes I got to know after I moved to Nashville.

In 1974, Bobby was on a roll, having started the year with his first number-one song. Written by Shel Silverstein, the song, "Daddy What If," was recorded with his six-year-old son, Bobby Jr. Its poignant lyrics, in which a son asks his father important questions, couldn't help but tug at your heart. On the album *Lullabies, Legends and Lies*, Bobby Sr. remarked that one day, when Bobby Jr. is older, he might sue his father for making him do it. His mom, Jeannie Bare, told me that when Bobby Jr. was in school at Belmont University, some of the students put the song on the speaker system in the cafeteria while he was eating lunch so they could razz him.

He never sued, and now, that little boy is having big success on the Alternative record charts as Bare Jr., with his first release, "You Blew Me Off." His manic style and loud music are quite the opposite of his father's laidback ways, making me wonder if this is his way of getting back at Daddy. What if?

This page: Bobby Bare and son perform at Fanfair (1995); facing page: Diamond Rio, Lee Roy Parnell, Steve Wariner and Radney Foster are among the participants who performed on Arista's Mama's Hungry Eyes Merle Haggard tribute album (1994).

Conway Twitty

One of the most prolific artists in country music was Conway Twitty. Starting on the pop charts with "It's Only Make Believe," in 1958, Conway had over fifty number-one hits, including more than forty on the country charts. A total of sixty-six songs made it into the top five, a number that will be impossible for anyone to beat in any musical genre.

During the five decades that he performed, he amassed a fortune and a following of fans that were the envy of most other artists. He was a star of the

first magnitude. On top of that, he was a truly nice guy.

I didn't have the opportunity to meet him until the early '80s, when I worked with photographer Dennis Carney. Dennis did several of Conway's album covers and other art during that time period, so he came by the studio quite often. Conway loved coming up with the concept covers Dennis was able to capture. Sometimes, it would take days to create the sets needed for these photos. The most complicated involved re-creating Norman Rockwell's masterpiece, "Self- Portrait," and making it fit with Conway's career. The results were magnificent, and we had a lot of fun doing it.

In the midst of it, Conway told us the funniest story on himself. It seemed that, a few years earlier, he'd been booked on a convention job at the last minute and didn't know much about who he was entertaining. Since he wouldn't wear his glasses onstage, he couldn't see the audience very well. At the time, he was opening his show with "Hello, Darlin'," a song that always received a strong round of applause from his fans. He heard nothing. He could tell that there were people out there, but they were just looking at him. When he finished, there was very little applause. That made him nervous. But he kept going.

At the end of the next song, there was still no response. He began to sweat. Maybe someone was playing a joke on him, he thought. Trooper that he was, he kept going and finished the show. He came off the stage totally confused. He soon found out that the

This page: Bobby and Jeannie Bare enjoy an autumn day at their home in Hendersonville, Tennessee (1987); facing page: Makeup artist, Vanessa Sellers, prepares Conway Twitty for an appearance on the Music City News Awards (1983)

audience was made up of mostly Japanese businessmen who couldn't speak English and didn't know who he was. He was also told that applauding a performance was not customary. He laughed and said, "I thought I'd lost my touch."

A year or so later, Conway needed another cover for an album. He came out to Dennis's studio and sat in the lobby looking through books filled with model photos. He didn't see anyone who fit his idea, so he went to a modeling agency to look at their books. Finally, he found who he wanted and brought her photo back to us. Everyone got a big laugh out of his selection, because all the while he'd been looking through our files, a giant portrait of her was hanging on the wall behind him. He had chosen one of our favorite people, a beautiful Kentucky lady named Naomi. A year later, he tried to get her for another project, but she and her daughter, Wynonna, had been signed by RCA Records and were about to be stars. As the Judds career took off, I'm sure he got a big kick telling the story about the model who got away.

Conway's sudden death in 1993 shocked and saddened the entire industry. With Loretta Lynn at his bedside, Conway succumbed to complications after a blood vessel burst in his abdomen. The day of his death, Mark Chesnutt was supposed to unveil a billboard celebrating the release of a new album. MCA Records canceled the ceremony, saying this was not a day to celebrate.

In 1994, Conway received one more CMA nomination for his work with Sam Moore on MCA's

Rhythm, Country and Blues album. Their version of Brooks Benton's classic "Rainy Night in Georgia" is probably one of the finest works of his long and illustrious career. Though it is sad to think of what else he might have recorded, his body of work will keep him around forever.

Mickey Gilley

Jerry Lee Lewis's cousin Mickey Gilley had a big hit with "Room Full of Roses," establishing a very successful career that continues today. He always has a vase of roses on the piano when he performs. Interestingly enough, he was on the Playboy Records label, and even recorded a duet with playmate Barbi Benton. During the Urban Cowboy phase of country

music, his club, Gilley's, was featured in the movie of the same name, helping him continue his string of hits well into the '80s. He later opened a club in Branson, Missouri.

Mel Tillis

In 1976, Mel Tillis was well on his way to being named Entertainer of the Year by the CMA after more than twenty years in the business. While many of the songs he had written, like "Detroit City" and "Ruby," were hits for other artists, he'd had consistent chart action with songs of his own, including "Who's Julie" and "The Arms of a Fool," achieving his first number-one with "I Ain't Never," in 1972. Aside from his musical abilities, Mel's one of the funniest people in country music. Though he has a bit of a stutter when he talks, his can send an audience into fits of laughter when he tells a story. He's also been a successful publisher with many hits, including Dwight Yoakam's first number-one, "Honkeytonk Man." His children kept a watchful eye on what Daddy was doing for a living, and all pursued music careers. His boy Sonny is a songwriter, his daughter Carrie April is an opera singer, and daughter Pam

went on to win a CMA trophy of her own for Female Vocalist in 1994. Unfortunately, Mel missed the award show because he was in Branson, Missouri, entertaining at his theater. He was part of a very funny album, called *Old Dogs,* with his friends Bobby Bare, Jerry Reed and Waylon Jennings.

Waylon Jennings

Speaking of Waylon, this was also the time when he was having great success. His rebellious spirit made him a natural for inclusion on an RCA album called *The Outlaws,* with Willie Nelson, Tompall Glaser and his wife, Jesse Colter. This collaboration started a movement within the industry that brought in a lot of rowdy, long-haired performers—and an audience that looked much like them. Artists like David Allen Coe and Johnny Paycheck also began appealing to this crowd. These were wild and rowdy days.

George JONES

This page: George Jones attends a birthday party for country legend, Ernest Tubb (1979); facing page: George Jones and his wife, Nancy, who really is "the rock that he leans on" (1993).

When you ask many of the new kids coming up in country music who was a major influence on their desire to sing, one name comes up almost every time. Male or female, those on the horizons of country music say George Jones. From his former wife, Tammy Wynette, to Faith Hill and Patty Loveless, from Randy Travis to Garth Brooks and Alan Jackson, everyone sings his praises. It would actually be easier to list those who don't claim him as an influence than those who do.

From "Why, Baby, Why" in 1955 to 1998's CMA award-winning duet with Patty Loveless, this Texas boy has had radio hits in every decade. He has stubbornly fought to stay active in this business, despite his own bad habits along the way and the industry's desire for younger and younger artists. With his song "I Don't Need No Rockin' Chair" he threw down the gauntlet to those who wanted him to politely retire. Supporting him in that effort, in the song and its video, were many of the young kids that were expected to fill his "retired" shoes. When the song won CMA's Vocal Event of the Year, the honor was shared with Vince Gill, Garth Brooks, Joe Diffie, Patty Loveless, Mark Chesnutt, Pam Tillis, Alan Jackson, T. Graham Brown, Clint Black and Travis Tritt. They were, to steal a line from Minnie Pearl, "just so proud to be there."

The video also included boxing great George Foreman, who was also being called "over the hill" at that time. He delighted in being a part of this project, and despite his intimidatingly massive size and reputation inside the ring, he soon proved to be a sweetheart to work with when there was no punching involved. The two Georges got along very well, cracking each other up throughout the shoot. Nobody there considered these guys as washed up or retired. We were all in awe.

In March 1999, Mr. Jones was almost killed in a car wreck near his house in rural Williamson County. He was on his way home, talking excitedly on his cell phone to his stepdaughter about his new recordings, which he'd just heard. Distracted and not wearing his seat belt on this winding road, he

Tammy Wynette and George Jones were able to get past their divorce and become great friends (1995).

ety. A grand jury found that he'd been driving while impaired, and he was ordered to pay a fine and to enter an inpatient alcohol treatment program. He took full responsibility for his actions and apologized publicly for what happened. He called the accident his "final wake-up call" in his fight to lead a sober life.

Thankfully for all his fans and friends, George has

hit a concrete bridge railing just two miles from his house. His stepdaughter heard the whole thing over the phone, and, soon she, the rock that he leans on, was at his side. In an interview the day after the accident, Nancy Jones remarked how stubborn he was. "If he wasn't a fighter, we wouldn't be here today. This is the strongest man I've ever known." Maybe that's something else about him that makes him such an inspiration.

It was discovered that, unfortunately, George had been drinking. A small bottle of vodka was found under the passenger seat. No one knew that he'd fallen off the wagon after many years of sobri-

been recovering from the ordeal very well. Though still weak at the time of this writing, he had announced that he was to be on the road starting in June, and was including appearances at Fanfair on the Asylum Records show and at the Ryman Auditorium in August. His new single, "Choices," received strong airplay in the wake of the accident, and his album was released in July. Obviously, his fans have accepted his apology and, once again, have forgiven him for his mistake. Everyone is hopeful for his full recovery and thankful that the "Possum" is singing again. Country music wouldn't be the same without him.

One night, after Bobby Bare played the Exit In, I was among a group invited to go to Tomplall Glaser's studio to hear the new single he was releasing, written by Shel Silverstein. Single releases then had a song on each side of the 45 rpm record. The "A" side was considered the radio release, and the "B" side was there if anyone wanted to listen to it. That evening they were trying to decide which song would be the song they promoted to radio. As we listened to the songs, Waylon kept poking his head in the door, asking Shel for help on a song he was writing down the hall. He'd say "Shel, I'm stuck." Then Shel would give him a line, and Waylon would dash down the hall to put it on paper. A few minutes later, he'd be back for more advice.

I never heard what song Waylon was writing that night, but the ones we heard by Tompall and Shel were released a few weeks later. Radio was encouraged to play the ballad as side A, but DJs soon flipped the record to play the side we liked, a tongue-in-cheek song called "Put Another Log on the Fire," which quickly was nicknamed the "male chauvinist national anthem." Though it only made it to number twenty-one on the *Billboard* charts, it still makes me laugh.

Don Williams

Don Williams quickly became one of my favorites. His low, mellow voice and wonderful songs always made me turn the radio up. I didn't realize until a few

Waylon Jennings makes a rare appearance at Fanfair (1990).

years later that I'd already been a fan of his when he was in a group called the Pozo Seco Singers. Don hooked up with a young producer in Nashville named Allen Reynolds, who'd been a banker until he wrote a major pop hit called "Five O'Clock World." "Cowboy Jack" Clement had encouraged him to come here and work with him. Allen quickly helped Don and Crystal Gayle on their paths to stardom, just like he helped artists like Kathy Mattea and Garth Brooks several years. This led to Don winning CMA's Male Vocalist award in 1978. He's had several nominations along the

way, including one for Single of the Year, in 1984, for the song "Good Old Boys Like Me," which remains my favorite Don Williams song.

In the mid-'80s, Don's manager, Chip Peay, called me and asked if I wanted to go to the Opryhouse to photograph Don with B. B. King. It seems that they'd been fans of each other's music for years, and though they'd spoken on the phone, they'd never met.

I was eager to take this job because their mutual admiration showed me how good music has no boundaries. The concert was wonderful, and after the show they met backstage. Don had brought a tape of the new project he'd just completed and B. B. was happy to receive it. I hope one day they'll record something together. I believe it would be worth hearing.

Hank Williams Jr.

Shortly after I moved here, I began to shoot jobs for MGM records, thanks to my friend Cheryl Gibbs, who at the time was working there. One day she called me and asked me if I wanted to go to Bowling Green, Kentucky, to an Airstream camper gathering at Beech Bend Park to photograph Hank Williams Jr. performing. Of course I said yes.

I got tickled when we arrived at all of these campgrounds filled with shiny aluminum trailers lined up. As we drove past them, I wondered how anyone could find their way home after the concert. Luckily, Hank's bus looked quite different. We could see it parked directly behind a small stage at the bottom of a hillside, so we found our way backstage quite easily. Out front, between the trailers and the stage, people were getting ready for the show, setting up their folding chairs and coolers.

Merle Kilgore, Hank's manager and surrogate uncle, opened for him, singing songs he'd co-written, like "Wolverton Mountain" and one of my all-time favorites, "Ring of Fire." After Merle warmed up the audience, Hank came out and opened with one of his father's songs. The crowd loved it. He played some of his own better-known songs and they applauded politely. Then he played a song that was more rocka-

This page: B. B. King and Don Williams meet for the first time (1989); facing page; Longtime manager and friend, Merle Kilgore, presents Hank Williams, Jr., with the award honoring the induction of Hank Williams, Sr., into the Alabama Music Hall of Fame (1985).

billy than country and the crowd seemed uncomfortable. He played every instrument onstage in one song, and they seemed unimpressed. As I stood among the audience members, taking photos, I heard some people boo him and saw crumpled up programs thrown toward the stage. All they wanted to hear was his daddy's stuff.

After the show, we went back to the bus. Merle was out in front of the bus supervising sales of records and souvenirs, which included records and photos of his father. We climbed up the steep steps into the bus and waited in the cramped living area that was the norm at the time. Hank, who had been in the back changing shirts and cleaning up, soon came out.

He went to the stairwell, where a fold-down table had been opened in the doorway. Hank sat on one of the stairs and started signing autographs. One by one, the buying fans shuffled past the door and offered up merchandise for his signature. A lot of it was his father's stuff, and more than once I heard someone ask, "Could you leave the Junior off?" I couldn't believe it! How rude could you get? But Hank did

Charley PRIDE

When Charley Pride sang his 1974 hit "Mississippi Cotton Pickin' Delta Town", he was painting a picture of his childhood. Coming from the tiny town of Sledge, in the heart of The Mississippi Delta, every phrase was a memory. Since my father's family came from that same area, I'd seen those little towns every time we went home to visit. As he sang, he took me back with him.

Somehow, Charley has defied all the odds. Growing up poor, he and his family really did pick cotton and he really did walk down dirt roads to get anywhere. But Charley knew there was a world out there, and he wanted to see it. He knew he could succeed if he tried, so he did. He first looked at baseball as a way out, and soon found himself playing in the Negro leagues. Oh, did I forget to mention that he was black? Well, I did mention that he defied the odds.

A few years later, after he'd gone into regular minor league play, Charley's baseball career took him to Montana where the road took another turn after he sang at one of the games. The people liked what they heard, and he liked the applause. Soon, he was playing in the local clubs where he was eventually heard by the great Red Sovine, who encouraged him to come to Nashville. Shortly after Chet Atkins signed him to RCA Records, he was on the road again, toward being a star.

Year after year, the fans voted Charley Pride their favorite at Fanfair, even after he left RCA. In the late 80's, Jerry Bradley, who been at RCA at the same time, signed him to Opryland's new label, Sixteenth Avenue Records, and the fans followed.

This page, top to bottom: Michael Peterson gets to meet Opry member Charley Pride on the night of his Opry debut (1998); Charley Pride makes an appearance on the TNN Music City News Awards Show (1998); facing page: Charley Pride works on his album "My 6 Latest and 6 Greatest" (1993).

what they asked. I wonder if any of those fans felt guilty later that year, when he attempted suicide.

A year later, Hank fell down a mountain while hunting in Montana and split his face in half. After many corrective surgeries and special glasses, he emerged as his own person, determined to make his own music. With the help of southern rock's finest players, including Charlie Daniels and Toy Caldwell, Hank turned the corner and connected with an audience his own age. As someone only three months younger than he is, I felt what he did made sense. His father's shadow was covering a talent that was capable of standing on its own. Like Charlie Daniels and Willie Nelson, when Hank Jr. finally got to make his own sound, he helped change the direction of country music.

In the '80s, Hank hit his stride. With the younger crowds he attracted, his concerts became more like parties. His abilities onstage excited a whole new generation who didn't know him as his father's son. Still, in the middle of the show, he would do one of Hank Sr.'s songs, and the new kids ate it up. Hank cranked up the volume, danced all over the stage and sang those songs with a lot of Alabama pride. His song "Young Country" told the story of the blending of musical styles that has greatly influenced our generation.

At the first *Alabama Music Hall of Fame Awards* in 1985, he proudly accepted his father's induction award on his behalf. Later that year, he picked up his first of three Video of the Year awards from the CMA

for "All My Rowdy Friends Are Coming Over Tonight." In 1987, "My Name is Bocephus," based on the nickname his father had given him, became the second of his videos awarded a CMA bullet. In 1989, he shared his third one with his father, along with the Vocal Event award for "There's a Tear in My Beer," built around one of his dad's scratchy old demos that had never been released before. No other artist has three CMA video awards.

But the CMA didn't stop there. His album *Born to Boogie* took the CMA award in that category in 1988, and in 1987 and 1988, they honored him with their highest award, Entertainer of the Year. During that time period, he also took home three ACM Entertainer of the Year awards, three video awards and the Vocal Event award for his collaboration with his father. The father-and-son duo also were honored with a Grammy for "Tear in My Beer," which was Hank Junior's first Grammy win.

In the late '90s, Bocephus's son Hank Williams III made his debut on the Grand Ole Opry. Wearing one of his grandfather's shirts, the newest Hank impressed the audience as he did songs that made his family famous. Backstage, he was greeted by folks who were there the night his granddad made his debut. Many of the ones who were there for his dad's debut were there, too. It must have been a strange night for him, trying to fill all the shoes that walked that stage before him. It was somewhat eerie, seeing the living proof of a family tradition. I have to won-

der if his children will one day find their way to the stage that helped make the family famous. I wouldn't be at all surprised.

John Denver : One of Nashville's Outcasts

Nashville owes John Denver a big apology. His hits in the 1970s transformed country into a big hit maker. He was accused of mimicking what was done here in Nashville, but in reality he represented country song-writing at its best. He went straight for the heart, with simple language that evoked true feelings. He didn't need Nashville's blessing to do what he did. But I really think he wanted it.

John Denver, Olivia Newton-John, the Eagles, the Byrds and others were affected by what they heard as children. They saw Roy Rogers and Tex Ritter as children, and they heard Johnny Cash and Tennessee Ernie Ford singing magnificent country songs like "Sixteen Tons" and "Ring of Fire," just like I did while growing up in the '50s and '60s.

It was an introduction, for us, to a style of music that came before us. What these artists did was incorporate their memories into the music that they were making. In doing that, they inspired respect for country music in a new generation, while the country music being made in Nashville was becoming closer to the pop music of the '50s.

Growing up country was becoming harder and

Top to bottom: Hank Williams, Jr., at Beech Bend Park in Bowling Green, KY (1974); Thirteen years after his controversial win, John Denver presents the CMA Song of the Year Award, which would go to K. T. Oslin (1988).

125

harder for those who had succeeded and now had big houses in the city. New kids were remembering their roots, while Nashville was creating music that was affected by the pop music of decades earlier. Dubbed "Metropolitan Country," it seemed to be trying to bury its roots.

At the same time, there was a problem with the kids who remembered where those roots were buried. The irony of rejecting John Denver as a true country boy is that it will eventually put him in the Country Music Hall of Fame, along with Woody Guthrie, a reject from another generation, whose country roots led him from Oklahoma to California into the beginnings of folk music, a music that reflected the origins of country music.

With the '80s came a new era in country music. It was dubbed the "Urban Cowboy" movement, after the John Travolta movie that helped spawn it. That movie showcased Gilley's, a club in Pasadena, Texas, and brought its stars, Mickey Gilley and Johnny Lee, sudden widespread fame beyond the country charts. Clubs with mechanical bulls popped up everywhere and everyone pretended to be cowboys again. Of course, most of them couldn't ride, which led to lots of humiliation and many injuries. After watching a Japanese tourist get wracked in a Nashville club, I chose never to get on one. I wonder if these machines were the inspiration for Conway Twitty's mid-'80s "Don't Call Him a Cowboy" (until you see him ride)?

Though some artists tried to capitalize on the urban craze, the wise ones chose to strike out on their

own. Lee Greenwood, on advice from Mama Mae Axton, moved to Nashville from the Nevada clubs he'd been playing to try for a major record deal. He soon landed a contract with MCA Records and teamed up with producer Jerry Crutchfield. They had a string of hits including "Ring on Her Finger, Time on Her Hands" and his first number-one hit, "Somebody's Gonna Love You." "I. O. U." brought him a Grammy for Best Male Country Performance in 1983. He also picked up the 1983 CMA & ACM Male Vocalist awards, and was honored with the CMA trophy again in 1984.

But it was his patriotic ballad, "God Bless the USA," that catapulted him to super-stardom. It was soon being sung on ball fields and military bases all over the country. Lee was invited to tour for the USO and even made it to the White House. The Republican Party was quick to grab it as their theme song, and CMA voted it Song of the Year in 1985. His career was in high gear, with four number-ones in a row in 1985 and 1986, starting with "Dixie Road." After many successful years as a recording and touring artist, Lee now has a theater near Dollywood, in eastern Tennessee, where he continues to entertain his fans.

Kenny Rogers

Kenny Rogers hit his stride in the late '70s with the 4-million-selling 1977 CMA Single of the Year, "Lucille," followed by Don Schlitz's Grammy-winning Song of the Year, "The Gambler," and CMA's Male Vocalist honors in 1979. Kenny also picked up Grammys for Best Country Male Vocalist in 1977 and 1979, as well as the Academy of Country Music's Male Vocalist for 1977 and 1978, and their Entertainer of the Year award for 1978.

All of this set him up for even greater success in the '80s. *Billboard* named his song "Coward of the County" top single of the decade, and his duo with

Dolly Parton, "Islands in the Stream," came in sixth. Even number twenty-five was his, with "I Don't Need You."

"The Gambler" spun off into a series of TV movies, with the later ones showcasing the acting skills of Reba McEntire & Travis Tritt. Kenny's Branson Christmas specials in the early '90s gave the budding talents of Garth Brooks and Trisha Yearwood a chance for national TV exposure. He also landed the hosting job for the *CMA Awards Show* in 1984, and again in 1987, where he and Ronnie Milsap had a chance to perform their number-one duet, "Make No Mistake, She's Mine," which later won a Grammy.

This page: Wynonna and Kenny Rogers make a video for their Christmas song duet "Mary Did You Know?" (1996); facing page: Lee Greenwood performs on the Music City News Awards Show (1983).

In the early '90s, Kenny turned his talents to roast chicken. As part of a press group, I ended up next to his family's table at the 1992 grand opening of Kenny Roger's Roasters in Branson, Missouri. When he asked what I thought, I pointed out that they had no bread for the dinners. When the location opened on West End in Nashville, I noticed they had yeast rolls and these wonderful little corn muffins.

One of my college mates has worked with Kenny for twenty-three years as a player and collaborator, and was cowriter of "Love or Something Like It." If Steve Glassmeyer hadn't graduated from Austin Peay State University when he did, there wouldn't have been an opening for a campus photographer. I was lucky enough to fill his slot as he went off to pursue his dream. Over the years, it's always been a pleasure to see him as I've covered Kenny's career.

In 1996, Kenny and Wynonna performed a beautiful Christmas duet called "Mary Did You Know?" for his Magnatone Records album. Backstage at 1997's Fanfair, Kenny was surprised with a giant wall of plaques and a special award signifying the sale of 80,000,000 albums worldwide. Recently, he spent a month at the 3,200-seat Beacon Theatre in New York City performing in *The Toy Shoppe*, a Christmas musical that he and Steve Glassmeyer wrote. With the success of that show, they've begun writing another, when they can get the time. Don't be surprised to see them back on Broadway.

By the way, Kenny's wonderful 1999 single and video, "The Greatest," came from Don Schlitz, the same songwriter who wrote "The Gambler."

Ricky Van Shelton

Ricky Van Shelton's career kick-started after Randy Travis proved to Nashville that the traditional sound of country music could sell. With his beautifully clear baritone voice, Ricky had ten number-one records between 1987 and 1991. He covered, quite capably, Jack Greene's award winner, "Statue of a Fool," and introduced new songs like "Keep It Between the Lines" to an audience hungry for true country music. The Academy of Country Music thought enough of him to name him New Male Vocalist in 1987. The CMA membership was impressed enough to honor Ricky with the Horizon award in 1988, followed by the Male Vocalist award in 1989.

But it was the fan-voted Music City Awards that has stood by Ricky when the music business seemed to lose interest in him. After voting him Star of Tomorrow in 1988, they were impressed enough with his work to give him their Male Artist award in 1989, 1990 and 1991, and named him their Entertainer in 1990 and 1991. Add to that Single and Album in 1989, Vocal Collaboration and Video for "Rockin' Years" in 1992 and Christian Country Artist in 1995, 1996 and 1997, and you've got an artist that the fans just won't forget.

Ricky Van Shelton has fun performing at Fanfair (1992).

George STRAIT

In a business where lots of artists dress themselves in Western attire, George Strait is one of the few who can honestly consider himself a cowboy. Having been raised on his family's ranch, he pursued a degree in agriculture from Southwest Texas State University while playing clubs in the evening. When he's not on the road, he can be found on his sprawling Texas ranch working the cattle and doing all the chores necessary to make that part of his life as successful as his recording career.

A couple of summers ago, he took time off from his touring schedule so he could go with his son, George Jr., as he participated in junior rodeo. Though he could've made lots of money performing for his fans, George considered his son's activities more important. Add to that the fact that he's been married to his wife, Norma, for nearly thirty years. To borrow a phrase from the Riders in the Sky, "Now, that's the Cowboy Way."

George tried and failed a few times as he

This page: My mother, Rosemary, enjoys watching George Strait, up close and personal, at the #1 party for "True" (1998); facing page; George Strait makes a rare Nashville performance at Starwood (1987).

explored Nashville's music scene, but thanks to Erv Woolsey, who remains his manager today, he landed a deal with MCA Records in 1980. His first single, "Unwound," made it to number six on the *Billboard* charts in June 1981 and, a year later, he had his first number one one with "Fool Hearted Memory." He hasn't stopped since. In 1998, he surpassed his idol, Merle Haggard, in number of CMA nominations received. With eleven wins, he is tied with an Oklahoma boy named Garth Brooks, who considers George a hero.

Sometimes, the fun of my job is very personal. My mother adores George Strait. When the boxed set came out, I bought her a CD player so she could play it. Every year, when his album comes out, I buy it and send it to her. Last fall, when I found out George was coming to Warner Chappell's number-one party for the writers of "True," I convinced her to come with me.

I introduced her to the writers, Jeff Stevens and Marv Green, and got her a seat down front. She enjoyed watching the ceremony, but wouldn't pose with George for a photo, so I stepped back from the stage to get them in the same frame. I knew she'd want proof of where she'd been, so I had a few extra prints made and gave them to her. Sure enough, a few weeks later, my Aunt Eleanor in Raleigh, North Carolina, mentioned in a letter that she'd received one from Mom. As long as George makes her happy, he's on my heroes list, too.

Clint Black

Clint Black closed out the '80s by taking home the CMA's Horizon award. His first album, *Killin' Time*, went double platinum and eventually spawned five number-one singles for him in the *Radio & Record's* country charts. No one had ever done that before on a debut album.

Clint enjoys what he does. I think he always knew it would be hard work, so he takes it as a challenge. He thinks about the songs he writes. As an old philosophy and English major, I find the subjects of his songs interesting and his knowledge of language impressive. Though he never went to college, he is degrees above many who did.

One story I heard about him was said to have taken place at Fanfair just after he became popular.

There was a bit of a feeding frenzy as he walked to the RCA booth. People pushed too close, and a security officer tried to hold one person back as Clint was going by. He could see what was going on and didn't like it. He stopped the officer, saying, "All she wants is a picture." He posed for her and greeted other fans, then went on to the RCA booth to sign autographs. As it should be.

When Clint and James Stroud, his producer, were working on his first album, James told him he'd give him his Porsche if the record went gold. Sure enough, by the time Fanfair of 1990 rolled around, the album had sold 500,000. Clint took time away from Fanfair to attend the ASCAP number-one party for his first two singles, "Better Man" and "Killin' Time." He and his cowriters, Dick Gay and Hayden Nicholas were all smiles as they received their certificates. After they were done, James Stroud came over and said, "Come with me." I followed as he grabbed Clint by the arm and led him out the door. We walked over to James's car. He said, "Well, Clint, it's yours," and handed him the keys to his Porsche. Clint was dumb founded, but James was true to his word. A couple of years later Clint gave the car back to his friend.

Clint's pairing with Roy Rogers was uncanny. They were about the same height, and when they smiled their eyes squinted alike as their cheeks went up. When Clint and Roy sang on the *CMA Awards* show, he looked out at the audience with a grin that

This page: Producer, James Stroud, presents Clint with the keys to his Porsche after his first album went gold (1990); facing page: Steve Wariner hugs his first gold record, I Am Ready (1994).

told us what he was thinking. His smile seemed to say, "Can you believe I'm singing with Roy Rogers?"

A couple of years later, after it became obvious he was interested in acting, I asked him if he would like to play Roy Rogers in a movie. He said he'd have to do a lot of learning before he would dare tackle that role. He has since starred in a made-for-TV movie with his wife, Lisa Hartman, about a legendary rodeo rider wrongly convicted of murder. It was obvious that he'd been honing his acting skills, leaving me to believe that he just might, one day, be able to tackle the role of everyone's hero, Roy Rogers.

Steve Wariner

A few years ago Steve Wariner put out a wonderful instrumental album called *No More Mister Nice Guy*. That might be the only lie he's ever told. Despite his attempt at acting tough, Steve is truly one of the nicest people in the music business. Of course he has

to be, for he was born on Christmas day, which also explains his middle name, Noel. He's also another one of the "triple threats": Like Merle Haggard, Vince Gill and Glen Campbell, he can do it all.

I first crossed paths with Steve in 1979 at a showcase at the Exit In. He was a charmer, with an ingratiating smile and a talent that was memorable. He had already signed a deal with RCA Records, where his mentor and friend Chet Atkins was giving him full support. He had worked in Chet's band for a while and loves to tell everyone that Chet fired him. Basically, Chet had seen a talent and felt it was time for Little Stevie Wariner to fly on his own. Mr. Guitar knew what he was doing.

Steve had his first hit, "Your Memory," in 1980, making it to number seven on the *Billboard* country charts. Another year later, "All Roads Lead to You" took him all the way to the top. He stayed with RCA for a few more years, showing off his guitar talents on "Midnight Fire" and, ironically, on his last single for them, *Why Goodbye*. He surfaced a few months later on MCA Records and stayed with them for several years, having a string of hits including one of my favorites, "Life's Highway." His recording of "That's How You Know When Love's Right" with Nicholette Larson garnered Steve his first CMA nomination in the 1986 vocal duet category.

Respect for Steve's abilities continued to grow. He picked up his first CMA award as part of Mark O'Conner's 1991 Vocal Event of the Year win, along with Vince Gill and Ricky Skaggs, for their great ren-

Alan JACKSON

Facing page: Alan Jackson performs as the headliner at Fruit of the Loom's Country Fest outside of Atlanta, Georgia (1996); this page: Actor, Hal Smith, better known as Otis Campbell on The Andy Griffith Show, meets Denise and Mattie Ruth Jackson during the making of the video for "Don't Rock The Jukebox" (1991).

the Jukebox, his second album, released in 1991, did even better. The video for the title song included two of Alan's heroes as guests, George Jones and Hal Smith, who played Otis Campbell on the *Andy Griffith Show*. Both albums were declared platinum by the RIAA that year, and the fan-voted *Music City News* awards gave him three of their statuettes at their June awards show. When one of our local radio stations decided to change formats from rock to country, they chose this song as the first one to be played.

Since then, his popularity has continued, with concert tours that invariably sell out, and albums of such quality that their release is always anticipated by fans and critics alike. In 1993, "Chattahoochie," a song he wrote with Jim McBride, became the big hit of the summer. It told a wonderful, rollicking story about playing along the waters of a beautiful river in the days of his youth near his hometown of Newnan, Georgia. It went on to grab all kinds of awards, including Single and Video of the Year from the CMA. The video taught the world that Alan Jackson was a very capable water skier—in cowboy boots, no less. His beautiful home on Center Hill Lake is evidence that he still loves the water. By the way, his boat is called the Neon

In 1989, when I walked into the offices of the newly formed country division of Arista Records to make head shots of the staff, one of the first questions I asked was, "Who have you signed?" Without hesitation they said, "Alan Jackson. He's gonna be a star." They raved about the tall, good-looking Georgia boy, pointing out that not only could he sing, he was a great writer as well. Boy, did he prove them right!

His first single, "Here in the Real World," a song he wrote with Mark Irwin, who was a bartender at the Bluebird at the time, rocketed to the top of the charts in April 1990. Before the year was over, he'd had two more number-one records, a best-selling album and several awards. *Don't Rock*

Rainbow.

In 1995, Alan finally reeled in the "big fish." As all of his albums reached multi-platinum status, the CMA awarded him the trophy for Entertainer of the Year. He followed that with the Academy of Country Music's award for Entertainer in 1996. In the summer of 1996, he became the headliner at Fruit of the Loom's 1st Country Fest at the Atlanta Speedway, not too far from his hometown. Along with Jeff Foxworthy, Hank Jr., Alabama, Pam Tillis and many, many others, he attracted 250,000 fans on a sweltering day in July. The Newnan, Georgia, boy had come home as the triumphant hero.

The year 1997 brought him a number-one hit with "Little Bitty," written by the storyteller himself, Tom T. Hall. Mr. Hall remarked that the first royalty check from this song was ten times the first one he received for his legendary "Harper Valley PTA," thirty years earlier. Tom got to watch Alan sing his song to a sold-out crowd at the new Nashville Arena, within sight of Tootsie's, where he used to hang out with his songwriter friends when he first moved to town.

Like Tom T. Hall, Alan Jackson has a career that will last a very long time. His consistency as a songwriter and performer has assured him a future

as one of the greats of this industry. Perhaps, one day, after Alan has slowed down, one of the songs he's written will be recorded by a hot new artist, and he'll find a check ten times the size of the first one he received for "Here in the Real World" in his mailbox. I believe it will happen.

This page, top to bottom: Alan Jackson proves he's a capable entertainer when he faces the audience, as well (1994); Alan Jackson accepts a bouquet at Fanfair (1992); facing page: Alan Jackson is quite often embarrassed by the applause he receives from women in the audience when he turns around on stage (1994).

Steve Wariner poses on his patio with two of his other passions, his wife, Caryn, and one of the watercolors he painted (1993).

dition of the song "Restless." That same year, Steve joined the roster of Nashville's hot new label, Arista Records. There, singles like Bill Anderson's wonderful song "Tips of My Fingers" kept Steve at the top of the charts.

In 1994, I got a panic call from the label, asking if I could come over on short notice. After adding in the sales from the record clubs, they had discovered that Steve's first Arista album, *I Am Ready*, had gone gold. Steve and his wife, Caryn, came to the offices expecting to be part of a sales meeting. Instead he received a surprise greeting by the entire staff and was presented with his first gold record. This was his first in all the years he had spent in the business.. Needless to say, Steve was thrilled. He hugged the album, then hugged everybody in the room. It was a delightful moment, watching a good guy win.

The year 1996 brought Steve an offer he couldn't refuse. After years of being a special guest on their show, Steve was asked by the cast of the Grand Ole Opry to become a member of the family. His album *No More Mr. Nice Guy*, with special guests like Chet Atkins, Larry Carlton and Boz Skaggs, had just been released to rave reviews, and Steve couldn't have been happier. He seemed to float through the evening of his induction with an amazed look on his face. He sang "Tips of My Fingers" with Bill Anderson and performed an instrumental with his hero, Chet Atkins, under the watchful eyes of Minnie Pearl, whose giant images loomed over them as part of an ongoing TV special.

But the next year, things seemed to bottom out, and he and Arista parted ways. Sadly, sales of his albums weren't going that well, and a couple of singles had fallen flat, so he was released from his contract. Label boss Tim DuBois was heartbroken, because Steve was also a good friend. Disappointed, Steve turned heavily to songwriting and began to work on his own project in his home studio. His wife,

Caryn, who also ran his publishing company and fan club, began plugging his songs to other performers to keep the lights on. He also did a duet with Anita Cochran for her first album. "What If I Said" was so popular that radio began playing it because of listener requests. Her label, Warner Brothers, released it to great success, even garnering a CMA Vocal Duet of the Year nomination. What started out as a cloudy year was beginning to show some silver lining.

Then came 1998. Caryn's pitches paid off. Garth Brooks liked a song that Steve had written with Rick Carnes in a pop/rock style. Garth called and suggested that it might be good as a western swing song. Who were they to say no? Garth also asked Steve if he would perform on the cut. Who was he to say no? Then they found out that Capitol Records wanted to release it as Garth's first single off the long-awaited *Sevens* album.

"Long Neck Bottle" entered the *Radio & Records* charts at number seven and bounded to the top of the charts in five weeks. The album broke records, ending the year with sales in excess of six million units. In the meantime, Garth was lobbying heavily for Capitol's new label head, Pat Quigley, to give Steve a deal. After hearing Steve's homegrown project, Pat knew it was an offer he shouldn't refuse. The first single, "Holes in the Floor of Heaven," put Steve back on the top of the charts. The album, *Burning the Roadhouse Down*, with Garth adding his vocals to the title cut, became Steve's second gold record. The membership of the CMA was so impressed with

"Holes" that they named it Single and Song of the Year, putting Steve in seventh heaven.

Steve started 1999 still on a roll. At his gold record party, he sang one of his new songs for an audience at the Ryman that included a live radio feed that went out to the world. Calls for the songs poured into radio stations everywhere, and Capitol Records was forced to rush the release of the single. "Two Tear Drops," written with Opry mate Bill Anderson, is a two-hankie tearjerker from the unique perspective of the teardrops.

Once again, Steve the songwriter is shining through. His songwriting abilities have just led to four Academy of Country Music nominations, with "Holes in the Floor of Heaven" receiving Single, Song and Video nods, and the duet with Garth receiving one for Top Vocal Event. For Little Stevie Wariner and his very happy publisher, Caryn, 1999 is a very good year.

Billy Ray Cyrus

I want to say up front that I admire this kid from Kentucky. After struggling for several years playing small clubs, Billy Ray Cyrus hit town in a storm of excitement that would have consumed most artists. "Achy Breaky Heart" burned its way up the charts like a prairie fire. After staying number one on the *Billboard* charts for five weeks, controversy over whether it was really country brought a lot of criticism that almost overshadowed this new talent in Nashville.

Some people thought he was smug because of the

overly serious photos they'd seen. In truth, his is a very respectful and caring person, active in many charity events, some of which he's helped happen. And he's always been appreciative of his fans.

At the Triple Platinum Party for his first album, "Some Gave All," as he came out to the presentation platform, he saw some of the uninvited standing outside the fence. One girl was crying because he was so close and it seemed she wouldn't have the chance to meet him. Though everyone was ready to start the ceremony, Billy broke away from the TV cameras and managers and bounded across the parking lot to meet the crowd first. We ran to catch up with him. He shook hands with several people and autographed a dollar bill for the sobbing girl. Only then did Billy head for the podium. When he finally got to the stage, she was smiling between her tears.

I had my first opportunity to meet Billy Ray in September of 1991, at a club called Night Life, near Opryland, where he was showcasing his talents for the executives of Mercury Records. They had a film crew and me to shoot stills, so they could see how he looked on camera. They were studying the raw talent, trying to determine what could make him a star. They never ordered any photos, they just studied the contact sheets.

A few months later, I saw him again at a Hank Williams Jr. party at the Ryman. Billy's manager, Jack McFadden, called me over, using the nickname he'd given me a few years earlier as we constantly crossed paths. "Hey, Scoop, I want you to take a picture of my boy with Hank." I had no problem with that. He took me over to Billy, who called me *sir* as we shook hands. We went over to Hank, and Jack introduced them. I snapped a few shots and delivered the photos a few days later. The screen went blank again.

Then, in April, a rumbling began on Music Row. "Have you seen that video of this new kid?" "Do you think it's country?" Then the grumbling. "Who does he think he is?" "Did you hear he was once a dancer at Chippendale's?" "What is it he's doing up there?" and "He'll never make it," were some of the comments I remember.

But Mercury Records had found a danceable country song that leaned in the direction of the rockabilly pop sounds of Memphis. "Achy Breaky Heart" caught on like the Twist did in the '60s. It was the kind of song that stuck to your brain and you either loved it or you hated it. Obviously, enough people loved it to send it zipping up the radio charts. The country dance clubs started teaching a special line dance created for the song. People were buying the album as fast as it could be stocked. Billy Ray had become a phenomenon. Still, most people had never seen him perform live, especially the folks on Music Row. Once again, it was like a big high school meeting the new kid in town.

When Fanfair rolled around in June 1992, Billy Ray was booked on the Mercury show, and the stands were absolutely packed. The Kentucky

This page: Tim McGraw shakes hands with fans at Fanfair (1995); facing page: Rock artist, Bryan Adams, joins Billy Ray Cyrus for an impromptu rendition of "Achy Breaky Heart" (1993).

Headhunters, Sammy Kershaw and the other performers had finished and the place was buzzing. Billy's band, the Sly Dogs, was in place and the sound system was being run through final check. The whole crowd, from the front row to the seats at the top of the stands, was looking at the stage with anticipation. If I had been in Billy's position at that moment, I would have been a quaking puddle hiding under the stage.

The Dogs started playing the intro to "Achy Breaky Heart," running the catch line over a few times, until Billy bounced onto the stage like a prizefighter. Every eye was on him. He danced out onto the thrust nearest the fans and stopped to look at them. You could see the amazement in his eyes as he tried to take it all in. He and the audience just looked at each other. Then he began to sing the song, and they went crazy.

More than twenty thousand people clapped and danced with him as he captivated them. Many of them already knew the other songs on the album, so they sang along on them as well. He ended the set as it began, with "Achy Breaky Heart." Though some people still wanted to criticize him, he proved to a lot of us that day that he was an entertainer. Later in the week, I was escorted through the throngs of fans to his booth to cover him meeting the fans. He talked to each one of them personally, looking them in the eye and wanting to know them as much as they wanted to know him. He had connected with the core audience of country music and, as Minnie Pearl would've put it, "He loved 'em back."

That first album, *Some Gave All*, exceeded eight million in sales by 1994, making it one of the best sellers in country music history. In the fall of 1992, "Achy Breaky Heart" picked up CMA's Single of the Year, surprising a lot of people in the audience and making Billy Ray the happiest boy in the world. As he and his producers, Joe Scaife and Jim Cotton, made their way to the stage, he grabbed the writer, Don Von Tress, out of the audience and dragged him along. Fans who had managed to get tickets were screaming from the balcony. Just as he did at Fanfair, Billy Ray looked around, trying to take it all in. You could tell he was still amazed. For a guy who had always seemed to look so serious, he had the biggest smile I'd ever seen.

Billy went through a few years of dead air when it came to radio airplay, but his fans kept buying his records and attending his shows. Last summer, at the 1998 *TNN/MCN Awards*, Billy Ray fans spoke loud and clear when he received the awards for Single, Song, Video, Album and Male Vocalist of the Year. He was dumb founded by the time he picked up the last one, running out of people to thank, except for the fans. He remembered them every time.

Since then, we've heard a lot more of Billy Ray on the radio. His single "Busy Man" climbed to number three before peaking in March 1999. As I write, his current single, "Give My Heart To You," and its video

are doing very well, something that, I'm sure, is giving Billy Ray Cyrus even more reason to smile. With the roll he is on, I expect him to do very well at the *TNN/MCN Awards* again this year.

Tim McGraw

When Tim McGraw's fifth album, *A Place in the Sun*, was released in 1999, it entered the *Billboard* Top 200 charts at number one, selling over 250,000 albums in the first week.

That wasn't the case with his first album, *Tim McGraw*, released only seven years earlier. It went nowhere, along with the singles Curb Records released to radio. Such a response would ordinarily doom an artist's career, but Mike Curb was patient

BROOKS & DUNN

This page: Brooks & Dunn celebrate their seventh #1 single with their producers Don Cook and Scott Hendricks and publisher, Donna Hilley (1994); facing page: Brooks & Dunn make their debut at Fanfair (1992).

When Tim Dubois ascended from songwriter and producer to head of Arista Nashville, he took with him his experiences "in the trenches." One of the first acts he signed was the Ray Benson-led Texas band, Asleep at the Wheel, one of the "darlings" of country music. Though they'd had no major radio hits, for years they'd built a following among cultivated country listeners, carrying on Ernest Tubb and Bob Wills's big-band country sound of the '40s and '50s. Tim loved their music and thought he'd found a song that would make the group a household word. The single was released and, despite their talent, it went nowhere.

that would make the group a household word. The single was released and, despite their talent, it went nowhere.

Tim was disappointed, but he still loved the song. Impressed with the talent of the writer, Ronnie Dunn, he felt Dunn should meet someone else he knew who once had recorded an album, for Capitol Records, that didn't exactly burn up the record bins. In the back of his mind Tim knew it would be great if Arista Nashville had a duo on its roster. One day, he had the chance to introduce Ronnie Dunn to Kix Brooks, and the rest is history.

After three number-one songs from their first album, *Brand New Man*, their fourth single became one of those country-music phenomena that everyone has in their dreams.

The song Tim had loved so much, "Boot Scootin' Boogie," became a career- making hit for the duo of his dreams, Brooks & Dunn.

Since then, pair has dominated the country duo category of every award-giving organization. Between 1991 and 1999, they sold nearly 19 million albums, to boot. Seventeen of their first twenty-five singles have gone number one. Now, that's what I call scootin'. They also have the unique distinction of being the only duo ever to win the Entertainer of the Year award from both the Country Music Association and the Academy of Country Music. They received Grammys for their performance of "Hard Workin' Man," in 1993, and for "My Maria," in 1997. During 1998 and 1999, they've been involved in a very suc-

cessful concert tour with Reba McEntire, climaxed by their number-one recording with her:"If You See Him/If You See Her."

But there's something else about Brooks and Dunn that's not reflected in all the awards and album sales, and that is that these guys just love to have fun. From their practical jokes to their Legends Car racing, from horseback riding to Kix's recent Jetski ride from Nashville to New Orleans, they're always up to something. Onstage they always have a blast, with Ronnie staying close to the microphone while Kix bounces around the stage like the Tasmanian Devil. Offstage, they are among the nicest people in the business, always ready with a joke and a smile.

Every year, as they pick up their awards, Brooks and Dunn joke about the possibility of the Judds getting back together. This coming New Year's Eve, their "fears" will be realized, as the girls reunite for a concert in Phoenix,

Chet Atkins is illuminated by the fan's flashes at Fanfair. 1975

Clockwise from left: Roy Acuff entertains The Opry audience by balancing his fiddle bow on his nose (1974); Minnie Pearl interviews customers outside the first Minnie Pearl's Fried Chicken (1969); Bill Monroe waves to the audience on the first night of Sam's Place at The Ryman (1994); The immortal Minnie Pearl is honored by The Opry after Sarah Cannon, her creator, passed away (1996); Boots Randolph & Danny Davis at the opening of the Stardust Theatre near Opryland (1995); Dolly Parton gives an awesomeperformance of "He's Alive" on the CMA Awards (1989); Roy Acuff adjusts the microphone for Opry legend Deford Bailey (1974).

Clockwise from top left: At the age of 80, Hank Snow performs on The Opry (1994); Kitty Wells receives the TNN Music City News Living Legend Award (1993); Randy Travis & Minnie Pearl at the 1987 CMA awards; Shania Twain showcases her talents on the CMA Awards show (1996); Hank Williams III makes his Opry debut in a shirt his grandfather once wore (1996); Billy Ray Cyrus sends "Achy Breaky Heart" to England via satellite (1992); Hanks Williams, Jr. is gleefully surprised with his 1st CMA Entertainer of the Year award (1987); Vince Gill, Earl Scruggs, Ricky Skaggs, Roy Husky, Jr., Marty Stuart & Alison Krauss showcase the fine art of bluegrass on The Opry (1994).

Clockwise from top left: The Judds perform on the CMA Awards show in the outfits they also wore in their finale concert (1987); Kris Kristofferson & Rita Cooledge sing together on In Concert's country series (1975); Dwight Yoakam & Buck Owens bring "The Streets of Bakersfield" to the CMA Awards show (1988); Mary Chapin Carpenter enjoys the response from the audience on the CMA's 35th Anniversary Special (1993); LeAnn Rimes makes her CMA Awards show debut (1996); Emmylou Harris, Kathy Mattea, Trisha Yearwood, Pam Tillis, Patty Loveless and Suzy Bogguss backup Mary Chapin Carpenter on the Women of Country Music TV Special (1992); Alan Jackson has as much fun as the audience at a lexington, Kentucky concert (1993); Keith Whitley showcases in a jacket that once belonged to Lorrie's father, George Morgan (1986).

Clockwise from top left: Tanya Tucker flirts with the Fanfair audience (1992); Alan Jackson sings for the first time at Fanfair (1990); Shania Twain returns to Fanfair just weeks after her album "The Woman in Me" goes gold (1995); Michelle Wright turns to direct the band at the end of "Treat Me Like a Man" (1992).

This page: George Foreman & George Jones enjoy working on the video for "I Don't Need No Rockin' Chair" (1992).

Facing page, clockwise from top: Brooks & Dunn proudly pose with their brand new Legends Cars (1993); Garth Brooks shows his love of baseball and charitable causes by playing at The City of Hope Softball Game (1993); The guys in Confederate Railroad play dressup for the "Trashy Women" video (1993); The Kentucky Headhunters show their support for Marty Stuart (1990) Tanya Tucker & her children celebrate at the platinum party for her album "What Do I Do With Me" (1992).

Facing page: The Dixie Chicks are totally ecstatic after receiving the CMA's Horizon award (1998).

This page, clockwise from top left: Alison Krauss & Union Station pose with their CMA Single of the Year award (1995); Trisha Yearwood beams proudly after finally receiving the CMA Female Vocalist of the Year Award (1997); Kathy Mattea is overwhelmed after her single "18 Wheels & A Dozen Roses" is honored by the CMA (1988); Vince Gill shows us his TNN Music City News Minnie Pearl Award (1993); George Strait picks up his first Entertainer of the Year award from the CMA in blue jeans and tails (1989).

This page, clockwise from top: Bob Dylan & Willie Nelson sing on the CMA's 35th Anniversary Special (1993); Roy Orbison awes a crowd of 30,000 in Memphis after Mercury's Class of '55 project was released (1986); John Prine, Bonnie Raitt & Tom Waits after their 1st time performing on the stage of the Grand Old Opry (1996)

It comes to no surprise that Farm Aid VI included some of the best talent available. Facing page, clockwise from top left: Lyle Lovett wears his Future Farmers of America jacket; A view of the stage and crowd; Nashville Diva, Jonelle Mosser makes her Farm Aid debut; Willie & Waylon; Farm Aid Founder Neil Young closes the show (1993).

Charlie Daniels shows us all why he chose Mt. Juliet for his home. 1989

This page: Kix Brooks & Ronnie Dunn bring their act to the Country Radio Seminar's New Faces Show (1992); facing page: Brooks & Dunn pose for a radio interviewer at Country Radio Seminar (1992); Ronnie and Kix pick up one of their many CMA Vocal Duo of the Year awards (1993).

Arizona. If the evening goes well, it won't be surprising if they play a few more dates. Still, I don't think the boys are worrying too much. Why, after the success of their recent "triette" with Reba, it wouldn't surprise me if they worked out something with the Judds, leading to the first tag-team duo in country music history. It wouldn't surprise me in the least.

and gave Tim the chance to record a second one. "Patience will out," they say, and in this case, patience has paid off for everyone involved.

Today, Tim is one of the most popular artists in country music. He now co-produces his albums with James Stroud and Byron Gallimore, and together they've become some of the best song pickers in town. The first single, "Indian Outlaw," from his second album (which was titled, ironically, *Not a Moment Too Soon*) became a big radio hit. The next single, "Don't Take the Girl," went to number one in *Billboard* and *R & R*, and later was honored with a CMA Single of the Year nomination in 1994. The

album became the best-selling country album of the year and opened the doors to a career that's still growing.

On another path at Warner Brothers Records that year was a young lady named Faith Hill. Both Tim and Faith appeared on the *Country Radio Seminar's New Faces* show in early 1994, along with Toby Keith, Clay Walker, Joy Lynn White, John Berry, Doug Supernaw and the Gibson Miller Band. Faith's first single, "Wild One," had topped the charts at number one in late 1993, just as Tim's single "Indian Outlaw" began its journey up the charts. Though they had met and were aware of each other's progress, they didn't know that their careers would eventually merge in a very special way. Nothing was further from their minds.

At the time, Faith was engaged to her producer, Scott Hendricks, and Tim had a steady girlfriend. Both performers had their noses to the grindstone, trying to launch their careers. Each was highly successful, with consistent top-five singles and million-selling albums. They were even nominated against each other for the CMA's Horizon award in 1994.

John Michael Montgomery took the award, but Tim and Faith continued their progress. Tim also received a 1994 Single of the Year nomination for "Don't Take the Girl," but lost that one, too, to John Michael's version of "I Swear," which had stayed at the top of *Billboard*'s charts for four weeks and on *R & R*'s for two. But by the end of the year, his album *Not a Moment Too Soon* was outselling John's by a million. Tim was on a roll.

In January 1995, Faith Hill's first album, *Take Me As I Am*, reached one million in sales, and her second album, *It Matters to Me*, was gold by November. Tim's third album, *All I Want*, was double-platinum by the end of the year, and *Not a Moment Too Soon* was then a quadruple-platinum success. Faith was again nominated for the CMA's Horizon award, but lost out to Alison Krauss's sweep of the awards show. By then, Tim was looking for an opening act for what he jokingly called the "spontaneous combustion tour," due to hit the road in 1996. He chose Faith Hill.

By the middle of the summer, there were rumors of a budding romance between Tim and Faith, neither acknowledged nor denied by the people around the two stars. During the August video shoot for Tim's upcoming single, "Maybe We Should Sleep On It," Faith was there, lending her support. It was obvious they were in love. The rumors continued to grow.

It was about that time that Tim's publicist asked me if I would be interested in going to Tim's hometown of Start, Louisiana, to shoot his charity softball game and concert, Swampstock. It would be on October 6, right after CMA week, and I thought it would be great to get out of town, even if it was only for a day. A week before the game, she called me and asked me to bring plenty of film, because we might do some family shots while I was there. I did as she requested and bought more film.

That morning, I took an early flight so I could get there in time for the game, which started at one in the afternoon. Several other people I knew were on the same flight, going to the game. It was obvious we were going to have fun. Among the artists who would be playing were Mark Collie, Kenny Chesney, and, of course, Faith Hill. I got to the hotel in plenty of time, thinking I could grab a bite to eat before going to the playing field.

As I picked up my key, I heard a voice behind me say, "Are you Alan Mayor?"

I turned to see a young lady wearing a lanyard with Tim McGraw "all access" badges on it. When I told her that I was, she said, "We need you right now." Not only did I not get something to eat, I never even went to my room. I took my bags to her car and we headed for the ball field.

When I got there, someone came up to me and said, "We need you at Tim's aunt's house right now. Tim and Faith are getting married." I just started laughing, realizing I'd been tricked into coming to this top-secret event. When I got to the house I realized I wasn't alone. Only a handful of people knew before we got there. Even the minister, the caterer and most family members didn't know until a few days before. Tim's band was as stunned as I was, but we were all getting a big laugh out of it.

None of the other artists or the press who were gathering at the ball field a mile a away had a clue of what was going on. To make sure there were no interlopers, the sheriff's department had a mounted patrol riding the perimeter of Tim's aunt's property. They were married in the backyard by the swimming pool. Faith was barefoot because she feared her heels would stick in the ground and she would fall down. Tim was the one with the big tears flowing down his cheeks. After the vows were said, Tim swept her off her feet and took her out to the tour bus so he could carry her across the threshold. After everyone stuffed their faces with crawdads, shrimp and catfish, and swapped stories of how soon they knew, we headed for the ball field to play ball.

Despite the desire for continued secrecy, Tim couldn't help but show off his new wedding ring to his friends who had come to play. At one point, as the TV cameras were beginning to circle him, I covered his hand and warned him. He quickly put his batting gloves back on and started the game. When reporters asked me if I'd heard that Tim and Faith had gotten married, I replied that I hadn't. It really was the truth. After all, I hadn't heard, I had seen them get married. At the end of the day, after all the TV crews had left and he was entertaining his hometown crowd, Tim let them know.

After singing a few songs, he said, "I would like to dedicate the next song to my wife, Faith." The crowd went crazy as he started singing, "It's Your Love." This time, she was the teary-eyed one, as she joined him onstage to sing her part. The people of his hometown stayed on their feet through the whole

Tim McGraw takes a little ride down on his Leipers Fork farm (1995).

song, with some of them wiping away their own tears. It was marvelous.

Since then, I have begun to call them the mushiest couple in country music. Every time I see them together, I see the special tenderness they have for each other.

As both of their careers have taken off, I've seen them beam with pride for each other's successes. It is when the accolades are shared that I see them at their happiest. Offstage, they are proud parents, sharing the duties of caring for their children, Gracie and Maggie.

It's not unusual to see one of them receiving an award while the other handles the children. Recently, at the dress rehearsal for Faith's tour, I joked with Tim about having to pull "daddy duty" while she put her show together. He smiled, and told me he'd had more fun than he'd had in ages, taking care of his girls.

Since their marriage, Tim and Faith's success has continued to grow. "It's Your Love" stayed at number one for six weeks and went on to be the Single of the Year in *Billboard* and *R & R*. The song, written by Stephony Smith, went on to pick up the CMA's Vocal Event of the Year award in 1997 and picked up the ACM's Single, Song Video and Vocal Event awards in 1998. Tim's album, *Everywhere*, which included "It's Your Love," won the CMA's Album of the Year for 1998.

Nineteen ninety-nine turned out to be Tim and

Vince GILL

Vince Gill performs on the CMA's 35th Anniversary Special (1993).

One of the most respected artists of the last two decades has got to be Vince Gill. He's what's known in the music business as a triple threat. In other words, he can write'em, pick'em and, my Lord, can he sing them. Truly one of the nicest guys in town, Vince has the love and respect of fans and fellow performers alike. And he's one of the funniest guys around, with a wit as fast as his fingers.

In the fall of 1998, after I almost burned my house down, I went to a Lila McCann studio session and ran into Vince in the hallway. He was working in another room on a project with newcomer Sonya Isaacs. My right hand was bandaged from the burns I'd received trying to carry a flaming frying pan out the back door, and he saw it right away. He asked what had happened, and I told him about the grease fire I'd accidentally started while trying to fry potatoes. After he knew everything was going to be all right, he couldn't help but mess with me by saying, "Don't you know fried foods are bad for you?" Then he smiled and patted me on the shoulder. I took no offense at his joke, because he was right. By helping me laugh at my foolishness, he helped me in dealing with it.

A graduate of the group Pure Prairie League, Vince was wooed by Mark Knopfler to join Dire Straits, but gambled on going country instead. In the early '80s, he found himself in Nashville working with Roseanne Cash and Rodney Crowell. He soon had an RCA Records deal that lasted a few years and did OK, but it wasn't till he hooked up with MCA Records that everything began to gel.

A gut grabber is a song so moving that your stomach starts shaking as you try to choke back the tears. Vince just might hold the record in this category. His skill as a songwriter was recognized starting in 1990, with the gut grabber "When I Call Your Name." Co-written with Tim DuBois, it defines the feeling of lonely. It picked up a Grammy for Vince's vocal abilities, and a Single and Song of the Year award from the CMA.

Next came "Look at Us," a song about a wonderful, long-lasting relationship that made you want to cry for all the good reasons. Co-written with the great Max D. Barnes, it picked up the CMA's Song of the Year in 1992. In 1993, they gave one of Nashville's premiere keyboard players, John Barlow Jarvis, a Song of the Year award for "I Still Believe In You," co-written with Vince Gill. In 1996, Vince picked up yet another Song of the Year award from the CMA for the ultimate gut grabber, "Go Rest High on that Mountain," written after the untimely death of his brother, and later sung in honor of his mentor, Bill Monroe.

Soon after, Vince wrote "My Pretty Little Adrianna," in reaction to the random murder of a 13-year-old girl in a shopping center parking lot. It went on to win a Grammy. In Nashville, the young lady who was killed, Adrienne Dickerson, has not been forgotten. The song raised our awareness of the

Left to right: Vince Gill compares his freshly shaved head with on of the kids participating at the Mini-Vinny golf tournament for children (1995); Vince Gill and his father are immortalized in bronze at The Little Course at Aspen Grove just outside of Franklin, Tennessee (1999).

senseless murders of children in this community. A memorial garden was planted in the memories of murdered children, and the Shop at Home TV Network established a memorial scholarship in Adrienne's name after they moved their headquarters onto the property where the murder was committed.

Vince has surpassed most of his heroes with the awards he's received, yet he remains one of the nicest guys in the business. To date he's picked up more CMA Awards than any other artist, including the Male Vocalist trophy five years in a row. He broke a record for all artists in all genres when he picked up a Grammy in 1999, making him the first to win one ten years in a row. Add to that his skills

at golf and basketball, which he has turned into charity fund-raising tools, and you've got one amazing human being.

In 1990, the first Vince Gill Celebrity Basketball Game and Concert was held at Belmont University, with the proceeds split between the athletic and music programs. The list of participants in the games reads like a Who's Who in the Nashville music industry. Vince has leaned on his friends and newcomers to fill the roster each year. Regular participants have included Rodney Crowell, Radney Foster, Linda Davis, Larry Stewart, Amy Grant, Tim Ryan, Ray Benson of Asleep at the Wheel, Kix Brooks,

Gary Chapman, members of Sawyer Brown, the Oak Ridge Boys, Diamond Rio and Baillie and the Boys.

Many others have participated in at least one game over the years. They include Garth Brooks, Reba McEntire, Barbara Mandrell, Travis Tritt, Billy Dean, Doug Stone, Emmylou Harris, Joe Diffie, Trisha Yearwood, Collie Raye, Faith Hill, Terri Clark, Leanne Rimes, John Michael Montgomery, the Sweethearts of the Rodeo and the Wilkinsons. The coaches have included Conway Twitty, George "Goober" Lindsey and Little Jimmy Dickens. And the list goes on and on. So far, they've helped raise nearly $400,000 for the school's scholarship programs.

In 1993, Vince lent his name to a golf tournament affectionately known as the Vinny. Once again, his name and reputation as a golfer attracted the best of the world of golf and music. This two-day pro-celebrity tournament, held at the Golf Club of Tennessee near Kingston Springs, has raised $1.5 million for a junior golf program in Tennessee, giving children who might not otherwise have had a such a chance the instruction and encouragement needed. Two facilities have been built with youth in mind, one at Golf House Tennessee near the Legends Course, and the Little Course at Aspen Grove, both near Franklin.

Vince gets a big kick out of seeing the kids have fun with a game he loves. Golf greats, like Payne Stewart and Fuzzy Zoeller, and serious amateurs, like Amy Grant and Garth Brooks, have played in the tournament since its inception. In 1998, a bronze statue of a father and son playing golf together was unveiled in Vince's honor. It was modeled on Vince's father and a ten-year-old Vince Gill.

Since 1992, Vince has been involved in hosting the *CMA Awards* television show.

In 1992, he cohosted with Reba and joked about how many costume changes she made. In 1993, he shared the duties with Clint Black, and since then has handled the three-hour show on his own. His easygoing style and rapier wit make the shows fun to watch between the performances and awards.

The 1999 Grammys once again showed the world the many talents of Vince Gill. He picked up his sixth Male Vocalist Grammy in a row, for "If You Ever Have Forever in Mind," a song that he also wrote. In another category, he shared the Best Country Instrumentalist Grammy with Randy Scuggs for "A Soldier's Joy." When he accepted his Male Vocalist trophy, he showed his sense of humor by holding it up to his ear and saying, "If you listen carefully, you can hear Garth Brooks playing baseball." Nineteen ninety-nine's wins tied him with Chet Atkins for most won by a Nashville performer. Odds are, in years to come, he will surpass his hero for the most Grammys. When he does, he will accept the honor humbly, then make a joke about it.

Faith's year. ACM and MCN/TNN honored both of them with their Top Male Vocalist and Female Vocalist awards. "Just To Hear You Say That You Love Me" received ACM's Top Vocal Event award in April, and captured Song of the Year and Vocal Collaboration of the Year in June.

Faith also received the Single and Video awards on both awards shows for "This Kiss." Her album *Faith* was certified triple platinum by the RIAA, as was her first album, *Take Me As I Am*. And for the final episode of its long-running television show *Mad About You*, NBC chose Faith's "The Secret of Life" for the ending.

Tim's recording of the Rodney Crowell/Will Jennings song "Please Remember Me" stayed at number one on the *R & R* charts for three weeks.

As the time of this writing, there is no doubt that the fall 1999 CMA awards will be very good to country music's most popular couple. Rest assured that Tim and Faith will be nominated in several categories, which will sometimes put them in direct competition with each other. No matter who wins, each will be proud for the other, but Tim and Faith will always be proudest of the awards they've received together—especially their two littlest ones, who probably will be asleep at home while their parents accept more.

Keith Whitley

Thinking about Keith Whitley always makes me sad. The guy finally had everything going for him

Keith Whitley flashes that infectious smile of his as he performs on the International Fan Club Organization's show (1987).

when he died suddenly, after drinking more alcohol than his system could handle at once. I was talking to a publicist about something that morning, when she said to me, "By the way, did you know that Keith Whitley died?" I thought she was making a crude joke and waited for the punch line. I questioned her. "No, really, he died," she replied. I hung up the phone and called someone I could trust who numbly told me the truth. Everyone on Music Row was shocked and hurt by this tragedy.

When I was growing up, the term *chug-a-lug* was filled with humor because of Roger Miller's description in his 1964 hit on Smash Records. After Keith's death, it wasn't funny anymore.

Apparently, after he had spent many days on the road, Keith downed a lot of alcohol in a very short time and then lay down to sleep . He never woke up. His wife, Lorrie Morgan, had just left to perform some dates in Alaska, and their children were with some of the family. No one was there to notice. By the time his brother stopped by a few hours later, it was too late.

Keith and his friend Ricky Scaggs had come up through the ranks of bluegrass music with the help of pioneer Ralph Stanley. Both of them were members of Ralph's band, the Clinch Mountain Boys, in the '70s. Both of them had desires to go further with their music. Only one of them made it.

Keith was a charmer with a warm smile and a strong, sincere handshake. In social situations, he made you feel comfortable—made everyone feel included—never acting like a star. Aside from his bluegrass raising, vocally, his influences were Texans Lefty Frizzell and Whitey Shaefer. His remake of their song "I Never Go Around Mirrors" clearly showed where he got the cry in his voice. His inclusion among the performers on Hank Williams Jr.'s 1986 single "Young Country" proved that everyone thought he was going to be part of the future.

His romance with Lorrie Morgan, which soon turned to marriage, showed up in the video that RCA Records did for *Homecoming '63*. As they danced through the high-school prom set, you would've thought it was old footage of them, the way they looked at each other. Later, he and record producer Blake Mevis paid Grassland Elementary for the use of its gym in the video with a check for the school's library fund.

In 1987, Keith and Lorrie became parents of a boy, Jesse Keith Whitley, named after his father. Lorrie's daughter, Morgan, from a previous marriage, joined them at the hospital for a family portrait the day after he was born. Though Lorrie was still tired and dealing with some pain from just having given birth, the four of them posed for a very joyous photo. Everything seemed to be falling into place.

Less than a year later, Keith would have his first number one, with Bob McDill's song "Don't Close Your Eyes." His next four singles also would go number one, including "I'm No Stranger to the Rain," which received CMA's 1989 award for Single of the Year. Sadly, he wasn't around for the last two number ones. Lorrie had to pick up his award for him at the ceremony, just like she was picking up the pieces of her shattered life. The next year, "'Til a Tear Becomes a Rose," Keith's duet with Lorrie that was finished in the studio after his death won for CMA Vocal Event of the Year. Once again, Lorrie had to pick up the award alone.

A tribute album put out a few years later revived the sadness of the loss, and Alison Krauss's version of Keith's "When You Say Nothing At All" brought her into the mainstream of country music. With a little studio magic, her poignant version was soon combined with Keith's recording and was played as a "duet" by many radio stations. Her version won Single of the Year from the CMA in 1995, and helped her in winning the Horizon and Female Vocalist honors as well.

Though Keith is gone, our memories of him remain vivid. He made a lasting impression on anyone who ever met him. For a new generation of singers, like Ken Mellons and Daryl Singletary, he was an inspiration. What he sang was marvelous, but what he never got to sing will always make us wonder. His song "I Wonder, Do You Think of Me" will always be a reminder that he'll never be forgotten. ◾

Randy TRAVIS

Only one artist has put his hands and feet in wet cement for the Music Valley Wax Museum's Walk of Fame twice. With his manager, Lib Hatcher, he came to Nashville from North Carolina in the early '80s as Randy Traywick. He landed a job singing and flipping burgers at the Nashville Palace just outside the entrance to the Opryland Motel. His popularity at that location led to his immortalization as Randy Ray. A few years later, he made his mark again, this time as a star named Randy Travis. His straightforward approach, influenced by George Jones and Hank Williams, helped put country music back on the track. Some of us believe that he helped save the genre. If nothing else, he proved that tradition sells, when sung by a real artist.

In early 1986, TNN produced a Warner Brothers Records TV special. The headliner was Hank Williams Jr., with new artists the Foresters Sisters, Pam Tillis and Randy Travis getting a chance for national exposure. The audience was filled with Hank's rowdy fans, so the place was rocking. They had to be coaxed back to their seats quite often. When it was Randy's turn, a large group of young fans rushed the stage. Startled, he seemed to take a step back from them, then looked over his shoulder

This page, top to bottom: Randy Travis sings at The Nashville Place where he once flipped burgers when he wasn't performing (1985); Randy Travis and Lib Hatcher are greeted by The Opry's Hal Durham on the night of Randy's induction to the cast (1986); facing page: Randy Travis makes his contribution to the Merle Haggard Momma's Hungry Eyes tribute album (1994).

as though he thought Hank or somebody else famous had come onstage. Their excitement was for him. He had made a connection.

That fall, the same year George Jones won the video award for "Who's Gonna Fill Their Shoes," Randy Travis took home the Horizon award. When Don Schlitz and Paul Overstreet went up to accept the Song of the Year award for "On the Other Hand," the stunned new star was invited to come up with them. The next year, they shared the same spot again with "Forever and Ever, Amen." He still had that look of disbelief in his eyes.

In the late '90s, as Randy explored acting, and just as it seemed he'd been eclipsed too early by the new talents coming up, he became the first artist DreamWorks signed for their venture into country music. Within a year, Randy Traywick/Ray/Travis had two more number-one hits and the continued respect of his predecessors, his peers and, I feel sure, a bunch of kids in the generations to come. Just think: A few years ago, George Jones was wondering who was gonna fill his shoes.

George Jones listens as Randy Travis sings the song that will become their duets on Randy's album Heroes and Friends (1989).

6 | WELCOME TO THE BUSINESS

Just how is a star made? It's a team thing. Lots of people are involved in this process. There's a manager who gets his percentage from what his artist makes. His job is to find jobs for his performer. These can be anything from a state fair to a movie deal. The manager who can make those connections for an artist who wants to do those kinds of things is a star in his own right. People gripe about the contract between Elvis and the Colonel, thinking 50 percent was way too much for the "hired help" to make, but Elvis is now an immortal, probably in a class with Julius Caesar and Shakespeare, from an historical perspective. So a good manager is probably worthy of compensation.

The producer is the guy who sits back and listens to the musical product as it is presented on a demo tape. This tape is the product of a publishing company whose writers have come up with a song tailor-made for the act that the producer is producing. Hopefully, they will convince somebody in A & R that the song should go to that artist or producer. "A & R" stands for artists & repertoire. An A & R person must have a good ear—one that satisfies the artist and the corporate bosses who breathe down his or her neck to find good product. On the publisher's side is the song plugger, who sorts out songs and tries to get these people to listen and record them.

This page, top to bottom: Deana Carter gets to meet Memphis producer Sam Phillips at a Capitol Records party (1998); Producer, Tony Brown, and Wynonna display their Ampex Golden Reel Awards for their album Tell Me Why (1995); facing page: John Jennings, best known as the producer of many of Mary Chapin Carpenter's albums, is also an accomplished musician in his own right (1994).

Of course, the demo tapes involve singers and musicians who are trying to get their start in this town—performers who, between waiting tables or selling boots, go to a studio and sing for their supper. Included among the best demo singers in this town's history are Janie Frickie, Joe Diffie, Kathy Mattea and Garth Brooks. They were willing to dig ditches in order to build the castles they had in their own dreams.

And then there is the engineer who knows all the bells and whistles in the studio to get the best recording possible out of all these various creative forces, in order to make them all happy, and to make something that the rest of the world loves as well. Following all of that come the radio and record promotion staff, who convince the world to accept this music that they obviously should love.

After all the songs are chosen and recorded, there are the manufacturers and distributors of the records. A few years ago, this part of the business was brought home to me by the appreciation Garth Brooks gave to the folks at the EMI Production plant in Jacksonville, Illinois. These people had produced every tape and CD that Garth had sold. At that time, the number was fifty million. The Chamber of Commerce representative pointed out that 800 families in that town owed part of their livelihood over the last five years to Garth Brooks. I saw him bow his head a little bit. Although it was a thank-you, it was also a realization of how many people depended on his success. Not only do you depend on them to make good records

for you, they depend on you, the artist, to make music good enough for them to keep manufacturing going. That's a lot of responsibility.

On the road, an artist depends on a road manager, who depends on a crew of drivers and roadies, sound and lighting techs and others needed to put on a good show. Gone are the days of station wagons and vans for most of the top acts in music. I once asked Narvel Blackstock, Reba McEntire's husband and manager, how many trucks and buses they were running that year, and he said, shaking his head, "They won't tell me anymore."

In another office is the publicist, who manages the news you hear about an artist. When an artist has a new album, a baby or a pickup truck endorsement, the publicist is the one who tries to let the world know. They clear photographers and reporters to cover the stories. By the same token, when an artist gets a divorce, is sued by a previous manager or shoots someone, the publicist is the one who has to fend off the press. As far as I know, none has had to deal with all three crises at once.

Add photographers, makeup artists, music video crews, costumers, merchandisers, caterers, security guards and fan club representatives, and you can begin to understand how much goes into the success of an artist today. A lot of people depend on an artist, and the artist depends on those people to make everything work.

To me, it's still amazing how anything really gets done. I'm convinced, in the end, that it's just magic

Producers, Ed Seay and Paul Worley, hold a rose in their teeth at a session for the group Wild Rose (1989).

that makes its happen. Putting all of the pieces of the puzzle together is beyond the scope of understanding. The responsibility that an artist assumes goes far beyond the songs we hear on the radio.

The Producers

The producers are the ears of the music industry. Usually, the general public only knows them as a name among the album credits, but what they do in weaving the instruments and voices together makes a big difference in the success of an artist. When Paul Cohen chose to produce records here in the 1940s, he became the first in a long line of producers who thought Nashville was the place to make records. Their abilities have had a lot to do with Nashville becoming a powerhouse in the recording industry.

It was Owen Bradley who helped convince Mr.

Cohen to utilize Nashville's musicians and the only studio in town, Castle Studio. He and his brother, Harold, soon built the second, and it wasn't long before Owen began producing the sessions himself. Decca Records soon began recording all its country artists here, from Red Foley to the great Patsy Cline, all under Owen's "watchful" ear.

Over at RCA Records, executive Steve Sholes felt the musical talents of a particular young studio guitarist made him a likely candidate to move into the producer's seat. After having played many sessions for the label in the 1950s, Chet Atkins began a career as an equally prolific producer. During his time at RCA, he produced many of the artists on the roster, including Eddy Arnold, Elvis Presley, Floyd Cramer, Boots Randolph, Don Gibson, Al Hirt, Connie Smith, Homer and Jethro and comedian Brother Dave Gardner. He also found time to produce all of his own albums at RCA, and when he moved to Columbia Records in 1982, he produced them as well—close to seventy in all. Of those albums, thirty were nominated for Grammys and twelve won. In 1993, Chet received a Lifetime Achievement award for his work as a performer and a producer.

The 1960s brought several producers to the fore-

front of country music in Nashville. Among them was Billy Sherrill, who headed Columbia Records. He showed ability as an executive by finding the talent, as a writer by writing many hit songs and as a producer of many of the label's most important records in the '60s and '70s. Among the songs he produced was the incredible ballad "Almost Persuaded," which he wrote with Glenn Sutton. The song garnered them a Grammy after Billy persuaded artist David Houston to record it. It remained at the top of the *Billboard* charts for nine weeks and was named the favorite country song of 1966.

Billy went on to sign and produce Tammy Wynette, whose songs "Your Good Girl's Gonna Go Bad" and "I Don't Wanna Play House" rocketed her to the top of the charts. The David Houston/Tammy Wynette duet, "My Elusive Dreams," also came from his writing and producing talents. His string of successes with Tammy continued into the 1970s and included the duets with George Jones, before and after their divorce. During this time, he also produced hits for Barbara Mandrell, David Allen Coe, Bob Luman, Sandy Posey, Joe Stampley, Freddy Weller and Johnny Paycheck, including Johnny's biggest hit, "Take This Job and Shove It."

Perhaps Billy's biggest successes as a producer involved two of country music's best-known male vocalists, George Jones and Charlie Rich. He was involved as producer and, in some cases, writer of Charlie's greatest recordings, including his three biggest hits, "A Very Special Love Song," "The Most Beautiful Girl" and "Behind Closed Doors." All three of those songs won numerous awards and helped Charlie Rich win the CMA's Male Vocalist of the Year in 1973 and Entertainer of the Year in 1974. Billy's 1980 production of George Jones's masterpiece, "He Stopped Loving Her Today," considered the number-one song in country music history.

Jerry Kennedy came to Nashville in the late '50s and soon became one of the area's busiest studio musicians. He worked with producer Fred Foster on many sessions, including Roy Orbison's "Oh, Pretty Woman," where he developed the guitar lick that gave the song its unique sound. He also worked on Shelby Singleton's pop projects that included Paul and Paula and Brooks Benton. It wasn't long before Jerry was producing his own sessions. That work paid off when he hooked up with a talented songwriter named Roger Miller.

The songs that the pair recorded for Smash Records, including "Dang Me," "Chug-a-lug" and "King of the Road," brought in eleven Grammys in 1964 and 1965. Jerry, by then the head of Mercury Records, was soon producing the Statler Brothers. His relationship with the group has continued throughout their recording career. Other artists he produced include Tom T. Hall, Jerry Lee Lewis, Johnny Rodreiguez and the Mercury recordings of a young Oklahoma girl named Reba McEntire. Among the productions of which he is most proud are his three sons, Gordon and Brian, who've written songs like "Change the World" and "American Honky Tonk Bar Association"; and Shelby, who is A & R director at Disney's Lyric Street Records.

Jimmy Bowen started his career as a performer in the group Rhythm Orchids, which had the big pop hit "Party Doll" in 1957. From there, he went on to work in a publishing company with a young writer named Glen Campbell. It wasn't long, though, before Jimmy found his true niche in the music business—as one of its most successful producers.

His first big success was with movie star Dean Martin at Reprise Records. "Everybody Loves Somebody," released in 1964, began a long string of successful singles and best-selling albums. Mr. Bowen's relationship with one member of the famed "Rat Pack" soon led to working with "Old Blue Eyes" himself, Mr. Frank Sinatra. Their recordings of "Strangers in the Night"; "My Way"; and "Something Stupid," the duet between Frank and daughter Nancy, were some of the most popular singles of Frank's career. During his California years, Mr. Bowen also produced up-and-coming acts like his friend Glen Campbell, Kim Carnes and Kenny Rogers and the First Edition.

In 1974, Mr. Bowen took over MGM Records and made several trips to Nashville to oversee the country

division offices. When the division was shut down by parent company Polygram, he moved to MCA Records, then, in 1977, to Electra/Asylum in Nashville, where he began producing country acts like Eddie Rabbitt, Crystal Gayle, Conway Twitty and Hank Williams Jr. When his company merged with Warner Brothers Records, he took over their operations in Music City. Within a year, he left them to take over MCA Records.

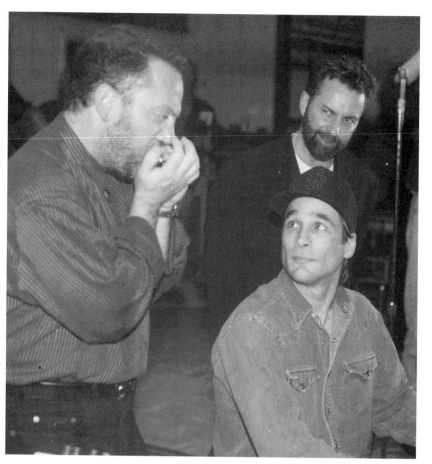

In the 1980s, Jimmy Bowen became known as the busiest producer in Nashville, working a whole roster of artists including Conway Twitty, John Schneider, Reba McEntire and a young Texas artist named George Strait. *Music Row* magazine named him Producer of the Year from 1982 to 1989. In 1989, he left to form his own label, Universal Records, where he had success with Eddy Raven, including the number-one single "Bayou Boys." His label also released the Nitty Gritty Dirt Band's *Will The Circle Be Unbroken, Volume Two*, which received great critical acclaim, a Grammy and a CMA Award in 1989.

It wasn't long, though, before Mr. Bowen shut down his label and took over the operations of Capitol Records, soon changing the name to Liberty Records. Although he still continued to produce some acts, he wisely allowed Jerry Crutchfield to continue producing Tanya Tucker, and knew better than to break up the magical pairing of producer Allen Reynolds and Garth Brooks. He produced newcomers Suzy Bogguss and Billy Dean, which resulted in gold records for both of them. He also brought John Berry to the label in 1993, where he, too, had great success. In addition, while at Liberty, he encouraged parent company EMI Records Group to purchase Gospel labels Sparrow and Starsong, creating a major powerhouse in Christian recording.

Perhaps Mr. Bowen's most important contribution to the music business in Nashville was to urge the studios to modernize, by moving from analog to digital recording technology. He knew what was happening in other markets and warned the industry that they would lose business if they didn't keep up. Within a couple of years during the mid-'80s, several studios including Emerald Sound, Sound Stage and Masterphonics had made the switch. Today, most of the studios continue to make upgrades in equipment as they become available. Mr. Bowen retired in 1995 after the removal of a cancerous thyroid tumor.

MCA Records' Tony Brown broke into the music business as a session player and keyboard player in the road band of Elvis Presley. He was also a member of the Oak Ridge Boys when it was a nine-member Gospel group in the early '70s. He began producing at MCA Records in the 1980s when Jimmy Bowen ran the label, working with acts like newcomer Steve Earle. When Jimmy left the label, Tony took over production duties of their already successful acts, like Reba McEntire and George Strait. He has since produced Wynonna, Vince Gill and most recently has taken over production of Trisha Yearwood's records.

Since 1990, Tony has been *Music Row*'s Producer of the Year three times. Since 1990, he has been nominated by the CMA for his production work on albums and singles twenty-five times. The album *I Still Believe In You*, which he produced for Vince Gill, won the CMA's Album of the Year award in 1993, and in 1996 and 1997, his George Strait albums, *Blue Clear Sky* and *Carrying Your Love with Me* also picked up that honor. The single "When I Call You Name," by Vince Gill, was his first CMA win in 1990, and in 1996, the George Strait single "Check Yes Or No" won that same award. Tony was also nominated for a Grammy as Producer of the Year in 1993, something unprecedented for a country producer.

Allen Reynolds first came to Nashville as a songwriter at the encouragement of legendary producer Jack Clement. He soon found himself at the production board with performer Don Williams at Jack's independent label JMI Records. The album that came out of those sessions, *Don Williams, Volume One*, received critical acclaim and produced two singles,

The BRADLEYS

I don't think you can properly explain the success of the music business in Nashville without talking about someone named Bradley. I have had the privilege, so far, of knowing three generations, and I've already met the fourth in diapers. The influence that they have had is absolutely amazing.

The best known is Owen Bradley, the producer of songs like "It Wasn't God Who Made Honky Tonk Angels," "Walkin' After Midnight," "Crazy," "Fraulein," "Jingle Bell Rock," "I'm Sorry" "Coal Miner's Daughter," "Hello Darlin'" and many others in the '50s and '60s. His artistry was so unique that k. d. lang sought him out in the '80s to produce her album *Shadowlands*, and

Mandy Barnett, with a voice often compared to Patsy Cline's, was the last artist to be helped by his skills in creating her album for Sire Records at the time of his death in 1996.

When Owen unexpectedly passed away, his brother, Harold Bradley, stepped in to help complete the album. For those who knew about the Bradleys, this was no surprise. The two of them had worked together from the beginning of the recording industry in Nashville, and before. Together, these Tennessee natives built some of the first facilities made especially for recording

This page: Owen Bradley, daughter Patsy Bradley, Bill Monroe and Owen's wife, Katherine, have fun at a BMI party (1993); facing page: Owen Bradley makes a rare public appearance on TNN's Music City Tonight for a Decca Records reunion (1994).

music that Nashville had ever seen .

Starting with a studio at Second & Lindsley in 1951—which made films as well as audio tracks of the sessions—they soon moved after the owner tripled the rent. The next studio was in an alley in Hillsboro Village, near the Belcourt Theater, which was the home of the *Grand Ole Opry* for a time during the 1930s. A few years later, they purchased a house on Sixteenth Avenue for $7500 and built a film and audio studio known as the Quonset Hut. The rest is history. From there, other studios began springing up, and the pool of musicians in what was becoming Music City began to grow. Harold and Owen remained two of the biggest fish in that pond. After they sold the Quonset Hut to Columbia Records in 1962, they built yet another studio in Mt. Juliet that would be known as Bradley's Barn.

Owen Bradley was the leader of his own dance band in the 1930s, moving quickly into live radio shows at WLAC and WSM in Nashville. Though WSM had three piano players on staff, Dinah Shore personally requested him as her piano player for the her radio show. After serving in the army during World War II, Owen came back to Nashville to continue his career. He soon became the studio leader for Decca Records' recording sessions and played on the first television broadcast for WSM in 1950. It wasn't long before he began his career as a producer of many of Nashville's most influential stars. The list of artists he produced is amazing. Included are Red Foley, Kitty Wells, Webb Pierce, Jimmy C. Newman, Brenda Lee, Jack Greene, Bill Anderson, Conway Twitty, Loretta Lynn and the immortal Patsy Cline. He was head of Decca and MCA Records from 1958 to 1976.

While Owen concentrated more and more of his time on production, Harold Bradley continued to play on sessions, racking up more time in recording studios than any other Nashville guitarist, exceeding even the great Chet Atkins. As of this writing, he is the president of the Nashville Association of Musicians, where he has been a member since 1942, working hard to protect the rights of musicians inside and outside the studio. He is a walking history book, with firsthand knowledge of Nashville's music business from the days of the big bands and radio orchestras through the latest high-tech studio work being done here.

Owen's son, Jerry Bradley, has followed in his father's footsteps, working as an executive at RCA Records in the 1970s; starting Opryland's label, 16th Avenue Records, in the 1980s; and serving as head of the legendary Acuff-Rose Music Publishing company. Jerry's wife, Connie Bradley, has been with ASCAP since the mid-'70s, and, as of 1999, serves as Nashville's vice president of membership, working on behalf of songwriters. Owen's daughter, Patsy Bradley, has worked for

While at BMI, Clay Bradley was involved with signing The Mavericks. l to r: Clay, former Maverick, Ben Peeler, Robert Reynolds, manager Frank Callari above Raul Malo, and Paul Deakin (1991).

over thirty years at BMI, where she started out as a secretary. Today, she is the senior director of publisher administration.

Harold's son, Bobby Bradley, is a well-respected studio engineer having worked in the industry for many years, and grandson Clay Bradley is now at Acuff-Rose after cutting his teeth at BMI for several years. With several great-grandchildren growing up in the business, there is no doubt that the Bradley family will continue to be an influence on Nashville music well into the next century.

"Amanda" and "In the Shelter of Your Arms." They soon followed with the second volume shortly before JMI closed.

Tony's next project was with Crystal Gayle on the United Artists label. Their first collaboration, *Crystal Gayle*, brought her good chart success, with songs like "Restless" and "Wrong Road Again." The second album, *Somebody Loves You*, helped launch her career, with singles like "Somebody Loves You," and her first number-one, "I'll Get over You." Tony and Crystal had continuing success with three more albums at United Artists. Long before the pop success of Shania Twain and Faith Hill's single "Don't It Make My Brown Eyes Blue" (written by Richard Leigh), they went all the way to number one on the pop as well as country charts. As a result, Crystal received the 1977 Grammy for Best Female Country Vocal Performance. Tony's production work helped her win the CMA's Female Vocalist of the Year award in 1977 and 1978, along with ACM wins in 1976, 1977 and 1979. When she moved to Columbia Records in 1979, she insisted that Mr. Reynolds continue as her producer, a relationship that lasted for several more years.

Allen's next collaboration was with a West Virginia girl named Kathy Mattea. Once again, he worked carefully to bring out the best qualities of a budding young artist.

After a couple of albums that didn't do all that well—partly because publishing companies weren't offering her the right material—they hit their stride with the album *Walk the Way the Wind Blows*. After her more mainstream version of Nanci Griffith's song "Love at the Five and Dime" made it into the top five on the country charts, the songs came rolling in.

The next album, *Untasted Honey*, resulted in her first two number-one songs with "Goin' Gone" and the wonderful "Eighteen Wheels and a Dozen Roses," which picked up the 1988 CMA Award for Single of the Year, as well as the ACM Single and Song of the Year. The next album, *Willow in the Wind*, included the tearjerker "Where've You Been," written by her new husband, Jon Vezner, and Don Henry. It received honors from the CMA, the ACM and a Grammy for Song of the Year, and Kathy picked up a Grammy and the CMA Award for her performance. Once again, Allen had done a great job at producing songs that brought out the best in an artist. Little did he know that the next one would be the mother lode of producing history.

When someone suggested that he listen to a tape by a new kid from Oklahoma, he agreed to—nice guy that he is—even though he wasn't seriously looking for a new act to produce. After hearing the tape and meeting with the artist, he agreed to work on a project with a determined young man named Garth Brooks. The rest is history. At the end of the twentieth century, the work he produced with Garth neared the 100 million mark in album sales, something that Allen never thought was possible, nor did anybody else. But that has always been a part of his talent, to understand the dreams and possibilities that the artist brings into the studio.

Working with Garth has been a challenge because his ideas continue to expand. Allen has listened to literally thousands of songs for each album, and together they've honed them down enough to fit. Allen has always accepted the challenges that Garth has offered, and come out smiling. To make the original cut of "The Thunder Rolls," Allen listened to many samples of real thunder and combined four to make the final recording. When they have cut the live tracks for the videos and live albums, he has been challenged with crowd sounds that were almost impossible to overcome. Still, Allen chose to overcome them rather than quit.

Perhaps, throughout it all, he still remembers a wonderful song Crystal Gayle recorded so many years ago, called "When I Dream," written by Sandy Mason and the title song of her fourth album, *We Must Believe in Magic*. Then again, he just might remember the song he wrote that was recorded by the Vogues in the 1960s and re-recorded by another artist, Hal Ketchum, whom he coproduced with Jim Rooney. Maybe the experience of working in the "Five O'Clock World" is what has kept him working so hard as a producer after all these years.

When James Stroud came to Nashville to work as a sessions drummer several years ago, he had no idea he would one day be working for Steven Speilberg and Jeffery Katzenburg of DreamWorks. Because of the "in-between" work he had done as a producer and then as head of Giant Records' Nashville office, James was asked two years ago to open the DreamWorks record label. As a result, he has found himself increasingly involved with Hollywood, including becoming executive producer of the Prince of Egypt's Nashville album. But James has done a lot to get where he is, and he's always done it without stepping on anybody's toes.

I first became aware of him as the drummer in a great band called the Kingsnakes, which consisted, in addition to James, of Wally Wilson, Glen Worf, Mike Henderson and Kenny Greenberg. Each one of them has become very successful in his own right. Wally Wilson has become a producer, working with people like Joan Baez and Linda Davis. Glen Worf consis-

tently has won awards for his bass-playing abilities from the Academy of Country Music and from *Music Row* magazine for several years in a row. Mike Henderson has recorded his own albums on the Dead Reckoning label and is a successful session player. He and Glen also are members of one of Nashville's most respected blues bands, the Bluebloods. Kenny Greenberg also plays sessions and produces records including one with his wife, Ashley Cleveland, that picked up a Gospel Grammy in 1999. James has surprised everyone including himself with his meteoric rise as a producer and as a record executive.

Though I had seen James perform, and had photographed the Kingsnakes' only recording session, I knew nothing about his interest in production until

it seemed like everybody was knocking on Mr. Stroud's door, asking him to become involved in their career. Since 1990, he has consistently been among the top five producers in town, according to *Music Row* magazine. They named him the top producer in 1994, as did *Billboard* magazine.

In 1992, James became president of Giant Records' newly opened Nashville offices, where he introduced us to the works of Clay Walker and Darlye Singletary. He also became executive producer of the album *Common Thread: The Songs of the Eagles*, which was named Album of the Year by the CMA in 1994 and sold over three million copies. He left that label in 1997 and went back to independent production. The other artists he has produced include Tracy Lawrence, John Anderson, Mark Collie, Carlene Carter, Lorrie Morgan, Pirates of the Mississippi, Doug Stone, Rhett Akins, Toby Keith, Regina Regina, Little Texas and Tim McGraw.

His coproduction work with Byron Gallimore and Tim McGraw on Tim's albums has paid off in a big way. The first four albums have exceeded twelve million in sales and the fifth entered the *Billboard* pop charts at number one when it was released in 1999. There have been twelve number ones so far, some of them staying on top for as long as six weeks. In 1998, they received the CMA's award for Album of the Year, for *Everywhere*.

1987, when I received a call to go to the studio where he was working with '60s pop performer Ronnie Dove. It was a small studio called the Downstage, and I was surprised to see him. Though that record didn't go very far, James was building up credits as a producer that would soon pay off. When Jimmy Bowen opened Universal Records, he asked James to be part of the staff. When the label folded James went back to independent production.

It wasn't long before he hooked up with a young Texas performer named Clint Black, and they began working on his first album. The first and second singles off that album brought them their first CMA nominations for Single of the Year in 1989 and 1990, and Clint picked up their Horizon award. After that,

When James Stroud took over the reins of DreamWorks Records, the first act he signed was Randy Travis. He also became his producer. Within months, they had the label's first number-one record, with the song "Out of My Bones." At the party celebrating their success, James reminded Randy that they first met when he was the session drummer on Randy's first album in 1985. It was obvious that there was a great sense of pride in having come full circle in his career. Look for more to come as he helps launch the careers of new performers Redmon and Vale, Jessica Andrews, Lisa Angelle and his newest signee, old friend Toby Keith.

I mentioned Byron Gallimore's work with James Stroud and Tim McGraw on Tim's albums, and I think it's necessary to tell you more about him, considering what all has happened in his young career. Byron grew up outside of Puryear, Tennessee, near the Kentucky border by the Land Between the Lakes State Parks. His family made a living farming, and he carried on the tradition. He learned about music while listening to older family members singing around the piano. Though he loved music, he never really considered it as a career—not at first. But after a couple of years of drought, he knew he had to look at other ways to survive. He decided to make his hobby into his profession.

When his early attempts at performing didn't go anywhere, he soon turned to publishing. After several years of working at Pride Music, he began to see that he would like to become a producer. In 1994,

that dream came to life when he teamed up with James Stroud and Tim McGraw. Since then, his pastures have become greener every year, growing by leaps and bounds. His friendship with James has led to the coproduction of Randy Travis and the new DreamWorks performer Jessica Andrews. He is also the producer of the Brooks and Dunn album, scheduled for fall 1999 as I write.

On a social trip in the early 1990's to a dinner club outside Puryear, Tennessee, Byron saw a young lady named Jo Dee Messina bring the audience to its feet. He was impressed with her, and soon began working to secure her a deal. He began passing tapes around Nashville and even took Doug Johnson, then at Epic Records, to see her perform. Her break finally came a few years later when Curb Records signed her, and he and Tim McGraw teamed up to produce her albums. Their work with Jo Dee has finally paid off with her second album, 'I'm Alright', going platinum, her 1999 Top New Female Vocalist award from the Academy of Country Music,and her nominations for the CMA's 1999 Horizon Award and Female Vocalist of the Year.

The projects with Tim soon led to Byron's producing Faith Hill, after her producer, Scott Hendricks, moved to Capitol Records and their relationship dissolved. Byron then teamed up with Dann Huff, once a guitarist for Amy Grant and many others in the Christian music field, to take Faith's career to phenomenal heights. The song "This Kiss" was a major crossover pop hit, and, as I mentioned earlier, the single "The Secret of Life" was chosen as the finale song for the television show *Mad About You*. The album they produced for Faith, appropriately named *Faith*, which included the single "This Kiss," broke the three-million mark in May 1999.

Dann broke into the business as a janitor at Sound Stage, where Jerry Kennedy did much of his production work. He had gone to high school with Jerry's boys, and was very interested in being a part of the music business. After many years of working as a session player, he entered into the production field at the suggestion of Shania Twain and her husband/producer "Mutt" Lange. By the way, as of 1999, Dann has had his own major number-one song as a producer of Lonestar's big single "Amazed" and, strangely, has had success with the metal band Megadeath at the same time.

And so the production process continues. There are many others who have made a living as producers whom I know and admire, and I hate to leave their names out. Fred Foster produced the first work on Dolly Parton and much of Roy Orbison's best work. As the head of Monument Records, he also gave the Gatlins, Kris Kristofferson, Eddy Raven and Barefoot Jerry a home for their music. Buddy Killen was responsible for the success of artists like Ronnie McDowell, Exile and Joe Tex, among others. Don Gant, Jim Vienneau, Shelby Singleton, Roy Dea, Bob Montgomery, Jim Fogelsong, Buzz Cason, Ron

Chancey, Jerry Bradley and Chip Young were also among the significant producers in the formative years of Nashville's music industry.

Jim Ed Norman has produced many great acts between his time in the mailroom and his rise to the presidency of Warner/Reprise Nashville, a job he has held longer than any other record executive in this town. They include the Eagles, Linda Ronstadt, Anne Murray, T. G. Sheppard, Kenny Rogers and Bob Seger. Garth Fundis was probably engineering the Ray Stevens song "Everything Is Beautiful," which I heard the first time I set foot in a recording studio— the one he now owns, the Sound Emporium. He has since been instrumental as a producer in the careers of people like Don Williams, Lee Roy Parnell, Keith Whitley, New Grass Revival and Trisha Yearwood.

Producer, Garth Fundis, works on a project with Trisha Yearwood and Lee Roy Parnell (1991).

Mae Boren AXTON

In all my years of meeting interesting and amazing people, few make it to the category of Mae Boren Axton. Best known as the writer of "Heartbreak Hotel" and as the mother of writer/actor Hoyt Axton, her influence on the lives and careers of hundreds of people has moved her into the category of legend. Because of her, Elvis had a major hit song, Willie moved to Nashville, Reba went to college and I got to photograph the legendary comedian Milton Berle.

Before my first encounter with this great woman, I had heard that she was pushy. I took that as a negative. To me that meant someone who had to have her way or else. What I discovered was that trait could actually be used for the good. Yes, she was one who wanted things her way, but it was usually for someone else, and, as far as I know, she was always right. She believed in other people's dreams and she did her best to help make them happen, and she was always on your side, even if you didn't find your dream.

In February 1979, I had the chance to photograph a surprise birthday party for Ernest Tubb at the Exit/In. That, to me, was exciting enough, but to go in and find that George Jones and many other famous people were attending was fabulous. I was still learning about this town, and this was a night of education.

Mama Mae was there, and I watched her work the room for the first time. She knew almost every-

This page: Mama Mae invites Peter Fonda to Ernest Tubb's birthday party in Nashville, so they could meet (1979); facing page: Son, Hoyt Axton, writer of Three Dog Night's "Joy to the World", with his mother, Mae Boren Axton (1996).

one and everyone knew here. Politicians and performers alike were there to honor Mr. Tubb, and the room was bustling with activity. Outside, a storm was covering Nashville with six inches of snow, but inside everything was warm and toasty. Some people were leaving, though, worried about getting home before the roads became treacherous. I was thinking about leaving, when my friend and fellow photographer Hope Powell said that she had to leave but that I should stay because of Peter Fonda. *With Easy Rider* still fresh on my mind, I thought that was unbelievable! Why in the world would he be coming to a country star's birthday party?

Well, I stayed. I looked out the door, and the roads were already white and dangerous, but what the heck. A short while later, who walked through the door but Peter Fonda. And who greeted him? Mae Boren Axton, a friend of the family.

She took him by the hand and walked him through the surprised crowd to meet Ernest Tubb. I took only a few shots of this event, and later found out that Fonda wanted to use some Ernest Tubb songs in one of his upcoming movies. He called Mama Mae and she made it happen. From that point on, I paid attention to what she did.

It wasn't till 1988 that I really began to understand her influence. I covered a fund-raising dinner in her honor for the Spina Bifida Association of America. Her sons Johnny and Hoyt were there, as were Willie, Reba, Waylon, Lee Greenwood and others. Those who couldn't be there sent in their toasts by videotape. Among them was her nephew, senator David Boren. One by one, they gave their testimonials about how she helped them in their endeavors. I began to understand what her existence meant to the rest of us.

In the '50s, Mae Axton was working as a publicist for "Colonel" Tom Parker, promoting shows for such performers as Hank Snow and a young kid from Tupelo, Mississippi, that Tom had just started representing. Tom asked Mae to look for material that the kid could do. She brought him a demo tape of a self-penned song made the way she thought

This page, clockwise from top left: Mae Axton greets many of her friends over the years: Andy Williams (1991), Willie Nelson (1985), Trisha Yearwood (1993), Garth Brooks (1994), Jack Greene (1988), and Waylon Jennings (1988); facing page: Mae Axton enjoys the fruits of her labor after helping Hollywood connect with Music City at Tammy Wynette's for Milton Berle's birthday. Left to right: Lorna and Milton Berle, Crystal Gayle, Mama Mae, Crystal's husband, Bill Gatzemos and Ray Stevens (1995).

Elvis should record it. "Heartbreak Hotel" set her up for life. Over 300 artists worldwide have recorded this song about the ultimate in lonely destinations. So, with this sad song, Mae Axton was able to become a positive influence on so many others.

In 1957, her work as a publicist would take her to Vancouver, Washington, to promote a series of Snow dates. She went to the local radio station,

KVAN, to be interviewed by a DJ who, with his new family, had moved up there from Texas. After the interview, he asked her to listen to some things he'd been writing, and though she needed to catch a plane, she took the time and listened. She was impressed. She advised the young man to move to Nashville. Willie Nelson soon brought his family and career here, and shortly thereafter his song "Crazy" helped establish Patsy Cline as a star. His stardom would finally come several years later, helping to change the face and hair-length of country music. He brought thousands of new fans to country music, widening its audience and making Mama Mae very proud.

In the early '70s, Reba's mother came to Mama Mae asking what to do with a precocious redhead of thirteen who wanted to be a star. She advised: "Let her finish her schoolin' first." Well, Reba com-

pleted college before pursuing her singing career, but didn't stop pursuing her education. Reba's continuing "schoolin'" made her a powerhouse in publishing and management, taking her far beyond her simple wish to be a performer. She told us at Mama Mae's funeral how much she appreciated her advice. She valued the friendship that came with it much more. They were friends to the end.

There are so many people, well known and unknown, who were helped by this wonderful woman. It was a source of pride to her that her friends did good. She looked out for them with a prayer and a phone call. She was insistent, yes—maybe even pushy—when it came to helping people realize their dreams, but it paid off for those who would follow through the doors she opened. It was up to them to turn her help into more. And when they made it, she was happy, just like a proud Mama should be.

After her funeral, everyone was invited to her house once more for food and conversation. She had left some money and a note explaining how it was to be used. "In love and appreciation for wonderful sons, grandchildren, other family and friends. Money for a 'get-together' of family and friends at my house after my funeral. Enjoy my hospitality…good food, good music, stories and happy conversation…. Because I've had such a great life, because of all of you! I love you all." Well, Mama Mae, we all love you. Thanks for making our world a better place.

As of this writing, songwriter Doug Johnson, who has worked with Ty Herndon, Rick Trevino, Doug Stone and John Michael Montgomery, heads Giant Records. He took over production of Clay Walker and coproduced the Wilkinsons' breakthrough album in 1998. Steve Buckingham, who produced several albums for Dolly Parton and has worked with Rick Trevino, David Ball and jazz artist Kirk Whalum, heads the legendary Vanguard Records office in Nashville. He also shared a Grammy win with Jim Henson for the soundtrack recording from *Watch That Bird*, starring Big Bird himself.

Keith Stegall has made a career out of producing Alan Jackson, after he coproduced Randy Travis's first album and stepped out of the second one to pursue his own recording career. When Alan came along he knew better. As of 1999, he was at Mercury Records and had added Terri Clark, Sammy Kershaw and Billy Ray Cyrus to his producing credits.

Jim Cotton and Joe Scaife got their big break when they got the chance to work with K. T. Oslin. The single "Come Monday" came out of that session and set

the stage for their next big project. Out of that came "Achy Breaky Heart" and a career for them and the artist, Billy Ray Cyrus. Nineteen ninety-nine found them working with Montgomery Gentry and Ty Herndon. Scott Hendricks has been involved in the production of records by Brooks and Dunn, Alan Jackson, Faith Hill, Trace Adkins and his first signee as president of Virgin Nashville, Julie Reeves.

Don Cook has brought success to the careers of Wade Hayes, the Mavericks, Brooks and Dunn and Alabama. Josh Leo has also worked with Alabama, as well as McBride & The Ride, Kathy Mattea, Michael Peterson and Paul Brandt. Barry Beckett has worked with acts as varied as Etta James, Bob Seger, Vern Gosdin, Lynyrd Skynyrd and Neal McCoy. Paul Worley has been instrumental in the careers of Martina McBride, Collin Raye, Pam Tillis and, with fellow producer Blake Chancey, the Dixie Chicks.

Legendary songwriter Norro Wilson teamed up in 1999 with another great songwriter, named Buddy Cannon, to produce three of the new kids in town. Their work brought number-one records for Chad Brock, Sarah Evans and Kenny Chesney, whose single "How Forever Feels" stayed at number one for six weeks on the *Billboard* country charts. Mark Wright has helped some of Nashville's new kids find their sound. They include Mark Chesnutt, Lee Ann

This page: Producers, Joe Scaife and Jim Cotton, with Billy Ray Cyrus (1992); facing page: Producer, Don Cook, seated on the left, with the group Lonestar (1995).

Womack, Gary Allan and Rebecca Lynn Howard. Mark Bright worked his way up from the tape room at EMI Publishing to a successful producing career with acts like Blackhawk.

In 1999, two artists who have had great success in their careers embarked on their first journey into the world of production. Vince Gill finished a project with his former backup vocalist, Sonya Isaacs, and Garth Brooks began production for an album by his longtime friend and bandmate, Ty England. I'm looking forward to hearing the finished products.

I have been intrigued by the many paths that have led to the job of producer. They have come from virtually every aspect of the music business. Songwriters, A & R directors, publishers, musicians and artists have moved into the producer's chair as Nashville's music business has evolved. The ears are everywhere, listening to what artists have to sing and helping them have careers. Without them, Nashville would never have earned the title of Music City, USA.

The Songwriters

In Japan, they have a poetic style called the haiku, which allows the writer only seventeen syllables to tell a story. In the music world, the challenge of writing a popular song has always been driven by radio's programming request of three minutes or less. The Nitty Gritty Dirt Band's immortal rendition of Jerry Jeff Walker's "Mr. Bojangles" drove me crazy because I thought it was too fast compared to what Sammy

Davis Jr. did with the same song on a television special. Many years later, when I asked Dirt Bander Jeff Hanna about that, he agreed with me but said they had to speed it up to get it on the radio. In concert they play it like it should be played.

Consider how many great stories you have heard on the radio, and think of what causes a writer to write a particular song. What was it that gave them the understanding of the topic? The answer is, simply, that the best songs have come from people who have lived them and are capable of telling their stories in a short period of time.

The greatest songwriters in country music history have got to be Jimmy Rogers and Hank Williams. As someone who came along after they were part of history, I was immediately affected by what they had written. Somehow, they were able to tell a story that was timeless, in only a few minutes, and connect with me decades after they wrote them. Last century, a gentleman named Stephen Foster wrote "My Old

Kentucky Home" and "Way Down Upon the Swanee River," which told the story of the American people as they left their homes and headed west. Today, they are considered historical treasures and are among the first songs taught in school.

Nashville has long been the mecca for songwriters. A. P. Carter, of the Carter Family, gave us "Wildwood Flower" and "Will the Circle Be Unbroken" in the 1920s, and today they are known by virtually everyone. Merle Travis's "Sixteen Tons" and "Smoke, Smoke, Smoke," Redd Stewart and Pee Wee King's "Tennessee Waltz" and Cindy Walker's "Distant Drums" and "You Don't Know Me" still connect with us over fifty years after they were written. "You Are My Sunshine," written by Jimmie Davis (later the governor of Louisiana), is one of the most recorded songs in history. Who doesn't know Gene Autry's "Back in the Saddle Again" and "Here Comes Santa Claus"? And Fred Rose's "Blue Eyes Cryin' in the Rain," published in the 1940s, was the breakthrough song for Willie Nelson in 1974.

Willie Nelson's song "Crazy" was a major hit for Patsy Cline in 1961 and for Linda Ronstadt in 1977. In recent years, I've heard Trisha Yearwood, Leann Rimes, Mandy Barnett and many others claim a spiritual connection to this song. That song, along with "Night Life" and "Funny How Time Slips Away," are timeless in their emotion, and came from the experi-

ences Willie lived, then remembered in song.

When I was a kid in Wichita, Kansas, we visited a city nearby named Abilene to see the Eisenhower Museum. It was an enjoyable trip, but my impression of the town really comes from a song written by John D. Loudermilk. "Abilene" was a monster hit for George Hamilton IV in 1963, at least five years after I went there, and the picture it paints always makes me think nice things about a town I visited only once. John had already supplied Mr. Hamilton with his breakthrough pop hit in 1956, the classic "A Rose and a Baby Ruth," and his songs, "Waterloo," "Then You Can Tell Me Goodbye" and "Tobacco Road" are universally known. John is considered an influence by many of today's songwriters and artists, including Rodney Crowell, Roseanne Cash and Vince Gill.

Felice and Boudleaux Bryant are among the few husband-and-wife writing teams in country music. Their compositions were influential in the career of the Everly Brothers, with hits like "Wake Up Little Susie" and "Bye, Bye Love" topping both the country and the rock charts in the late 1950s. They were very prolific, writing over fifteen hundred songs for artists as varied as Buck Owens and Leo Sayer. Perhaps their best-known song is now one of Tennessee's official state songs. When you go to a University of Tennessee sports event, you are guaranteed to hear their classic "Rocky Top." They were inducted into the Country

Music Hall of Fame in 1991.

One of my all time favorites is the wonderful writer, Roger Miller. From wacky ditties like "You Can't Rollerskate in a Buffalo Herd" to poignant ballads like "Husbands and Wives", the songs that flowed from Roger's pen were always memorable. The first time I heard it, "Husbands and Wives" absolutely shook me, long before I knew anything about the experiences described in the song. Some people think of it as unfinished because it ended so quickly, but I've always thought that the brevity of the song expressed volumes about the subject matter. As in the world of marriage and divorce, after a brief musical interlude, he simply repeated it. In Japan, that would be called a double haiku. I consider it a masterpiece.

Kris Kristofferson came here in the mid-1960's after graduating from Oxford University and spending a few years in the army. He worked as a janitor and a bartender while he honed his skills as a songwriter. After much persistence he was able to get Roger Miller to record a song that has since been recorded by many others, including Janis Joplin. "Me and Bobby McGee" was a monster hit for her, just before she died, selling millions of singles.

Soon everyone wanted to record Kris's songs.

This page, top to bottom: John D. Loudermilk regales us with a story about writing one of his songs during a songwriter's show (1987); Songwriting greats Kris Kristofferson and Kim Carnes meet at the Harlan Howard Bash (1995); The great Gov. Jimmie Davis, co-writer of "You Are My Sunshine" one of the best known songs ever written (1992); facing page: Billy Joe Shaver makes his performing debut at The Exit-In (1974).

Johnny Cash captured "Sunday Morning Comin' Down" perfectly in 1969, and Sammi Smith recorded "Help Me Make It Through the Night," which went on to capture Grammys in 1971 for Kris's writing and her performance. Other memorable Kristofferson songs include "Lovin' Her Was Easier" and "Why Me, Lord," which he wrote with Marijohn Wilkin early in his career. Ray Price had a number-one hit with Kris's "For the Good Times" in 1970. Altogether, Kris had nine Grammy nominations between 1971 and 1990, taking home three awards.

The CMA has nominated him seven times, with "Sunday Morning Comin' Down" winning Song of the Year in 1970. Since the mid-1970s, he's been in several movies, including *Pat Garrett and Billy the Kid*, *The Rose* and *Lone Star*.

Tom T. Hall has long been called the "Storyteller" because of his songwriting style. "Harper Valley PTA" and "The Year That Clayton Delaney Died" were complete stories that came from his own experiences. Jeannie C. Riley's recording of "Harper Valley PTA" eventually sold over six million records. As a

recording artist on Mercury Records in the 1960s and '70s, Tom recorded hundreds of his own compositions. In 1996, his song "That's How I Got to Memphis" was a breakthrough hit for new artist Deryl Dodd, and Alan Jackson had great success with Tom's song "Little Bitty," showing that a good song is timeless.

To give you an idea of how much country music has grown, Tom T. received two BMI Millionare awards, in 1999, for radio airplay: one for "Old Dogs, Children and Watermelon Wine," which was released twenty-seven years ago, in 1972, and one for "Little Bitty," which was a number one record in early 1997.

When I moved to Nashville in 1974, I soon found myself listening to an amazing group of songwriters. Jack Clement, better known as "Cowboy," not only wrote some incredible songs—like "I Know One," recorded by Jim Reeves and Charley Pride; and "Guess Things Happen That Way," which was a big hit for Johnny Cash in 1958—he also influenced the

careers of many other songwriters and artists. Starting out in Memphis, where he worked with Sam Phillips during the heyday of Sun Records, he went on to work with Carl Perkins, Roy Orbison, Jerry Lee Lewis and many others. When he moved to Nashville, he became Charley Pride's producer and supplied Bobby Bare with songs like "Miller's Cave." He continued to work with Johnny Cash into the 1980s, contributing many songs and producing some of his Mercury projects. He encouraged the young writer of "Five O'Clock World" to move here, where he became one of the city's most successful producers.

Left to right: Don Schlitz stops by Mississippi Whiskers, a songwriting hangout, three nights before getting his Grammy for "The Gambler" (1979); Songwriter, Jimbeau Hinson, and his wife, Brenda, spend lots of time out at the family farm, Beaufield (1987); Rodney Crowell has fun with his daughters after a songwriter's show (1987); Tom T. Hall sings some of his children's song for kids gathered at Nashville's Cumberland Museum (1988).

Allen Reynolds, who worked with Don Williams and Crystal Gayle in the 1970s and Kathy Mattea in the 1980s, was later sought out by a young kid from Oklahoma who wanted Allen to produce his first record. Nearly 100 million albums later, Garth Brooks still depends on Mr. Reynolds to make his country albums. Garth Fundis, who later produced albums by Keith Whitley, Trisha Yearwood and Lee Roy Parnell, engineered on many of those early projects.

Among the other writers Jack Clement encouraged was Bob McDill, whose songs, like "Good Old

Boys Like Me" and "Amanda," were important hits in Don Williams's career. He has received seven CMA Song of the Year nominations so far in his career, including for the two just mentioned. Others include "Baby's Got Her Blue Jeans On," recorded by Mel McDaniel in 1984, and "Don't Close Your Eyes," by Keith Whitley in 1989. Jack supplied Alan Jackson with the megahit "Gone Country," which tells of the transitions he has seen as Nashville attracted songwriters from everywhere. That song was also one of his CMA Song of the Year nominations, and it helped him become BMI's Songwriter of the Year in 1995.

Dickey Lee, best known for his 1961 pop hit "Patches," was another one of the writer's helped by Jack Clement. Besides "Patches," he wrote "She Thinks I Still Care," which was a big hit for George Jones in 1962, staying at the top of the *Billboard* country charts for six weeks. Dickey went on to a very suc-

cessful career as a country artist, with songs like "9,999,999," written by Razzy Bailey, and the number-one hit "Rocky." In the world of songwriting, his illustrious career includes co-writing two songs that were nominated as CMA Song of the Year: "The Door Is Always Open," with Bob McDill, which became Dave and Sugar's first number-one song in 1976; and Tracy Byrd's hit "The Keeper of the Stars," with Karen Staley and Danny Mayo, which was nominated for that same award twenty years later.

One of the first songwriters I met when I moved here was Charlie Williams. He is best known for songs like "500 Miles Away From Home," which he co-wrote with Bobby Bare; "I Got Stripes," which was an early Johnny Cash hit; and "I Never Picked Cotton," recorded by Roy Clark in 1970. Charlie was

one of a number of multitalented people who moved to this city. When he was a KFOX disc jockey in the late 1950s, he supplied the liner notes for Willie Nelson's first album and later managed his publishing company for a while. He managed Bobby Bare for a number of years and was helpful in Billy Joe Shaver's career in the 1970s.

Charlie also was a talented actor, appearing in movies like *Next of Kin*, with Patrick Swayze and Liam Neeson, and in music videos like Restless Hearts' *Dancy's Dream* and George Jones's *The Old Man No One Loves*. He also was the writer and talent coordinator for the highly acclaimed early TNN show "*Bobby Bare and Friends*" in 1980 and '81. I'm proud to say that he was my friend, and along with his wife, Diane Dickerson, was among the most helpful people to me when I moved here.

One of the most talented songwriters I know is Bobby Braddock. He and Curly Putman wrote Tammy Wynette1s 1968 hit, "D-I-V-O-R-C-E," and the 1980 George Jones classic, "He Stopped Loving Her Today." Both songs were nominated for Grammies and CMA Awards. "He Stopped Loving Her Today" won the CMA Single of the Year in 1980, and Song of the Year in 1980 and 1981. In the 1990s it was named the number one country song in history by Country America magazine and by the BBC in Great Britain.

His songs "Texas Tornado" and "Time Marches On" were number-one singles for Tracy Lawrence on the *Billboard* charts. "Time Marches On" was later nominated for the CMA's Single of the Year in 1996, and Song of the Year in 1996 and 1997.

Texas has supplied Nashville with a number of memorable songwriters, including Jerry Jeff Walker, Guy Clark, Billy Joe Shaver and Townes Van Zandt. Jerry Jeff's "Mr. Bojangles" has been recorded by a variety of artists from Sammy Davis Jr. to the Nitty Gritty Dirt Band. Guy Clark has written such hits as "Desperadoes Waitin' for a Train" and "L. A. Freeway," and has been a major influence in Vince Gill's writing career. Billy Joe is well known for John Anderson's song "I'm Just an Old Chunk of Coal,"

This page: Guy Clark receives the Lifetime Achievement Award from ASCAP (1998); Songwriting greats Bob McDill and Dickey Lee smile for the camera after a showcase at the Exit In (1979); facing page: Award-winning songwriters Hugh Prestwood, Mike Reid, Cheryl Wheeler and Beth Neilsen Chapman sing in the round at Nashville's best known listening room, The Bluebird Cafe (1988).

Harlan HOWARD

When it comes to Nashville songwriters, no one can beat the astounding record of Harlan Howard. Like the legendary Irving Berlin, who wrote thousands of memorable songs in the heyday of Tin Pan Alley, Harlan's prolific pen has written more than four thousand songs during a career spanning more than five decades. More than one hundred of these songs have made it into the Top Ten on the country charts. Several others have graced the pop and Gospel charts. Many of these songs were the breakthrough hits for up-and-coming artists.

Named after the city where he was born in Kentucky, Harlan grew up in Detroit, where his family moved at the height of the Great Depression, seeking work away from the coal mines. He grew up listening to the *Grand Ole Opry* and began to dream of writing country songs at an early age. After a stint in the army, Harlan decided to head for California to be a songwriter.

At the age of twenty-six, he got a job in the Los Angeles area so he could support his songwriting habit. He soon figured out how to get his songs to the people recording out there. With the help of people like 1999 Hall of Fame inductee Johnny Bond and artists Tex Ritter and Bobby Bare, he began getting cuts. By 1959, Harlan had found the mother lode of songwriting.

Charlie Walker took Harlan's "Pick Me Up on

Harlan Howard performs at the first Harlan Bash as his old songwriting buddy, Hank Cochran, looks on (1984).

Your Way Down" to number two on the *Billboard* country charts for four weeks in late 1958. In February 1959, Kitty Wells scored a top five hit with his song "Mommy for a Day." May brought a double success for "Heartaches by the Number," with Ray Price taking it to number two on the country charts, and Guy Mitchell taking it all the way to number one on the pop charts. Still, the royalties had not started coming in yet, so like any smart songwriter should, Harlan kept his day job as a forklift operator in a factory.

It is said that one of Harlan's bosses, who knew of his songwriting ambitions, was always ragging him about it. Harlan took it and kept on working. Then the checks started coming in. Within a matter of weeks he received nearly $100,000 in royalties, collected from the airplay of his songs.

Every day, he had seen this supervisor park his car in its reserved space. One day, when this gentleman rolled into his spot, he saw a car just like his in the next parking space. Standing there next to it was Harlan Howard. When the supervisor got out of his car, Harlan simply said, "I quit," got in his brand new Cadillac and drove away. Since then, though he's never had to look back, he's never forgotten his blue-collar days. That always has shown through in the songs that he writes.

It was during those struggling years that he met a Missouri girl named Lula Grace Johnson, who had moved to Los Angeles hoping to become a singer. It

wasn't long before they were married and raising a family. Under the name Jan Howard, Lula sang on many of the early tapes that later became hits, and soon had her own career. A number of her hits were with songs written by Harlan.

Together with their family they moved to Nashville in 1960. By 1967, she had a number-one hit with "For Loving You," which stayed on the top of the *Billboard* charts for four weeks. In 1971, Jan Howard was asked to join the cast of the Opry, a membership she proudly continues to this day. Sadly, though, her marriage to Harlan lasted only a few more years.

Shortly after moving here, Harlan had one of the biggest songs of his career. He and songwriter Hank Cochran created a song that would give Patsy Cline her first number-one country record. "I Fall To Pieces," which also climbed to number twelve on the pop charts, has gone on to be one of the most popular songs in history, and helped set a standard for female country and pop artists that continues today.

Harlan's country success was phenomenal. In 1961, he picked up ten BMI Awards, and at the 1962 BMI awards dinner, fifteen of the forty-one songs honored involved Harlan as a writer. Though many of his Tootsie's Orchid Lounge compatriots, like Hank Cochran, Willie Nelson and Roger Miller, were beginning to do well, he was consistently getting more cuts than they were. In 1963, a song that

reflected his tough beginnings became another big hit for him. "Busted" went to number thirteen for Johnny Cash and the Carter Family, but scored even higher—number four on the pop charts—for the rhythm and blues master Ray Charles.

Buck Owens, who bought the publishing to Harlan's early works, had a number-three hit with "Above and Beyond" in 1960, and decided to record an album made up entirely of Harlan Howard songs. Most of them are classics, including one he decided to re-record in 1965. That cut, "I've Got a Tiger by the Tail" stayed at number one on the *Billboard* country chart for five weeks, rising to number twenty-five on the pop chart as well. It was to become one of Buck's signature songs. Brenda Lee also hit the pop charts in 1965, with Harlan's song "Too Many Rivers" rising to number thirteen.

Harlan's old friend Bobby Bare released another one of his songs in 1966, which resulted in a top five hit. "The Streets of Baltimore," written with Tompall Glaser, captured a Grammy nomination that year, but was beaten by "Almost Persuaded." In 1967, Harlan provided Mel Tillis with a number-eleven song, "Life Turned Her That Way." This was highest he had ever charted in his career. Later that year, Waylon Jennings scored a top ten hit with "The Chokin' Kind," which was an even bigger hit two years later when released by Joe Simon, staying at number one for three weeks on the *Billboard* R & B charts. One by one, it seemed like all the artists were

Harlan hangs out backstage with some of his friends, including Lucinda Williams and Emmylou Harris (1994).

becoming indebted to Mr. Howard's special talent.

In 1974, at the height of his career, Charlie Rich's label released Harlan's "She Called Me Baby," which promptly climbed to number one. By then, Harlan had reached the status of elder statesman among Nashville's songwriters. The Nashville Songwriter's Association International had inducted him into their Hall of Fame in 1973, at the age of forty-four. Every new kid who came to town wanted to be like Harlan, and nervously sought him out for advice. Wherever he went, whether it was to a restaurant or a publishing office, others followed.

I had the opportunity during that time to be one of those people on a few occasions. These gatherings were always fun, filled with stories and lots of people. One afternoon, at a restaurant called Faison's, I noticed he was "holding court." One by one, people

would stop by the table to pay homage, from the kid who just got off the bus to Bill Ivey, who then ran the Country Music Foundation and later became the head of the National Endowment for the Arts. I realized that, if Elvis was the King of Rock and Roll, and Roy Acuff was the King of Country Music, then Harlan Howard was the King of Nashville's songwriters.

The 1980s brought Harlan continued success, with John Conlee dipping back into his old catalogue for the classic hit "Busted," taking it to number six in 1982. When he did it in concert, people began giving him dollar bills as he walked along the edge of the stage. John was amazed at this reaction, and soon began passing this money to charity, a practice he continues to this day. In 1984, Conway Twitty had a big hit with the charming song "I Don't Know a Thing About Love," and a new mother/daughter duo were thrilled at the chance to record one of Harlan's compositions. No one knew at the time that the Judds' name would soon become a household word. "Why Not Me" went on to win the CMA's

Single of the Year and the ACM's Song of the Year, and helped the girls win a Grammy for Vocal Duo in 1985.

The rest of the '80s included hits with Reba McEntire's 1985 cut of "Somebody Should Leave," which rose to number one. The Forester Sisters' remake of "Too Many Rivers," which climbed all the way to the top, and Highway 101's first number-one, "Somewhere Tonight," made 1987 a very good year for Harlan. Ricky Van Shelton's version of "Life Turned Her That Way" helped him win the CMA's 1988 Horizon award and garnered Harlan a Song of the Year nomination. The next year, Rodney Crowell scored a number-one song with the remake of the old Buck Owens cut, "Above and Beyond."

In 1984, Harlan became involved with one of the most fun Music Row events ever. What became known as "The Harlan Howard Birthday Bash" raised money for the Nashville Entertainment Association and the Nashville Songwriters Association International for twelve years. At his request, hundreds of the best songwriters and performers available took time to be part of the party. Among them were Buck Owens, Keith Whitley, K. T. Oslin, Mel Tillis, Pam Tillis, Brooks and Dunn, John Prine, Emmylou Harris, Nanci Griffith, Lucinda Williams, Kris Kristofferson, Michael McDonald, Donna Summer, Rodney Crowell, Tammy Wynette, Roger Miller, Kim Carnes, Ronnie

This page: Harlan surprises Buck Owens with a smack on the cheek (1988); Harlan's songwriting friends hoist his chair into the air at the end of the first Bash (1984).

Milsap, David Lee Murphy, Alabama, Guy Clark, Lyle Lovett, Chet Atkins, Carl Perkins and John Schneider.

The '90s continued to be good for Harlan Howard. With his cowriter, Max D. Barnes, he had the pleasure of supplying Pam Tillis with her breakthrough hit, "Don't Tell Me What To Do," just as he did for her father twenty-four years earlier. It rose to number five in *Billboard* and made it all the way to number one in *R & R*. Collin Raye's first single, "All I Can Be" came from Harlan, as did Chely Wright's, but the highlight of the decade—of Harlan's career, in fact—was his 1997 induction into the Country Music Hall of Fame.

He looked dapper that night, in his tux and with the cane he needed after recent back surgery. With a twinkle in his eye, he expressed his gratitude for the award, but let us know he was most proud of the fact that it was going to a songwriter. That night, he got the chance to show the world the honesty and sense of humor that many people in the music industry have gotten to know through the years. He also let everyone know that he had no plans to rest on his laurels. He knew that when he started out in his day job, and he certainly wasn't going to do it now.

He and his wife, Melanie, started their own publishing companies, signing several promising young writers, gambling on their talents to carry them through. In 1998, they helped the W. O. Smith School of Music raise money at the Hard Rock Cafe with a concert billed as "Harlan Howard Unrocks the Hard Rock." As always, he was able to call upon his friends to help out. This time, they included Terri Clark, Vince Gill and Waylon Jennings. Once again, he packed the place with song lovers willing to pay top dollar to help the future of the music community.

Harlan and Melanie's publishing ventures paid off when their writer, Rory Lee, scored his first number-one hit with Collin Raye's single, "Someone You Used To Know," co-written with Tim Johnson. They are also hoping for singles out of songs included on new albums by Lorrie Morgan and Clay Walker. In 1999, Harlan's pen has been busy, too, with cuts by Sara Evans and Joe Diffie.

At age seventy, he was still writing regularly with the cream of the "juveniles," as he fondly calls the younger writers. As Nashville moves into the twenty-first century, Harlan Howard is nowhere near giving up his crown, and, personally, I don't know anyone who is ready to take it from him. On behalf of everyone who's ever met him, or was moved by one of his songs, I say, "Harlan, you're the greatest." Long live the King of the Songwriters.

"Honky Tonk Heroes" by Waylon Jennings and "Old Five and Dimers Like Me." He and his son, Eddie Shaver, have worked together for years, at the time of this writing in a band appropriately called Shaver.

The great Townes van Zandt remains one of the industry's most revered songwriters, with many friends and fans in the business, including Nanci Griffith, Emmylou Harris, Willie Nelson and Garth Brooks. His song "If I Needed You" was a successful duet for Emmylou and Don Williams in 1981, and "Pancho and Lefty" was a huge song for Willie Nelson and Merle Haggard in 1983. Both songs garnered the artists Grammy nominations for Vocal Duo or Group. Townes's stories were always chillingly honest portrayals of people going through hard times.

Don Schlitz moved to Nashville in the 1970s, making some money from tip jars in clubs like Mississippi Whiskers and the Exit/In, though his day job as a computer operator really paid the bills while he tried to break into the business. He soon lucked out when the muse visited him one night and a song called "The Gambler" was born. Several people recorded it before Kenny Rogers heard it and made it into a major hit in 1979. Don got a Grammy, a CMA Song of the Year award and a career as a major songwriter from that version. And it didn't hurt Kenny's career either.

Don Schlitz's songwriting helped Randy Travis's career too, by supplying two songs he co-wrote with Paul Overstreet. "On the Other Hand" and "Forever and Ever, Amen" captured the CMA's Song of the Year awards in 1986 and 1987. Don went on to be ASCAP's Songwriter of the Year an unprecedented four years in a row, from 1988 to 1992, and Paul Overstreet has since been named BMI's Songwriter of the Year four times, as well.

My friend Jimbeau Hinson has had a long string of hits from songs he has written since Brenda Lee

This page, top to bottom: Songwriter, Don Von Tress, accepts a TNN songwriter award for "Achy Breaky Heart" with singer Billy Ray Cyrus standing proudly in the background (1993); Trisha Yearwood celebrates her #1 single, "Perfect Love", with the songwriters Stephony Smith and Sunny Russ (1998); facing page: Wild Texas writer and mystery novelist, Kinky Friedman, hugs his old friend Chuck Glaser of the 1960's group The Glaser Brothers after a show at The Bluebird Cafe (1998).

recorded "Broken Trust" in 1980. While that song peaked at number nine, his next one was a major hit for the Oak Ridge Boys. "Fancy Free," one of their best songs, was the follow up to "Elvira" and made it all the way to number one. In 1986, MCA Records chose a song Jimbeau wrote with Steve Earle for Steve's first single release. Though it only went to number thirty-seven in *Billboard*, "Hillbilly Highway" helped start Steve's career as a performer. Kathy Mattea took Jimbeau's "Train of Memories" to number six in 1987, which helped pave the way for her next release, "Goin' Gone," her first number-one record. David Lee Murphy had the good fortune to meet Jimbeau in the early 1990s and began writing with him. Though it stopped on the radio charts just short of a number one, R & R named their song "Party Crowd" Single of the Year for 1995.

Garth Brooks has had the good fortune to work with many great cowriters over the years. Among those who have written with him on a regular basis are Kent Blazey, Kim Williams, Pat Alger and Victoria Shaw, as well as his wife, Sandy Mahl Brooks. The hits they wrote together include "If Tomorrow Never Comes," "Papa Loved Mama," "The Thunder Rolls," "Unanswered Prayers," "The River," "That Summer" and "Ain't Goin' Down Till the Sun Comes Up." A

This page, top to bottom: Mickey Newberry sings "American Trilogy" on the Noon Show, a song that Elvis later recorded (1972); Max D. Barnes picks up the CMA's Songwriter of the Year award for "Chiseled in Stone", co-written by the singer, Vern Gosdin (1989); facing page, left to right: John Michael Montgomery happily poses for a photo with Steve Diamond, Jennifer Kimball and Maribeth Derry, the writers of the ASCAP Song of the Year, "I Can Love You Like That", which he recorded (1996); Lyle Lovett performs on a TNN tribute to songwriting great Roger Miller (1997).

very fine writer named Tony Arata supplied him with "The Dance," and the team of Earl Bud Lee and DeWayne Blackwell were lucky enough to have their song "Friends in Low Places" heard by the then unknown Mr. Brooks at a songwriter's showcase at the Bluebird Cafe.

Another songwriter who's had the opportunity to write with Garth is Mark D. Sanders. Their collaboration resulted in the song "Victim of the Game," which was included on *No Fences*, and "Whatcha Gonna Do With a Cowboy," a hit duet for Garth and Chris LeDoux. Since then, Mark's been a cowriter on a phenomenal string of hits by many artists. Among these are John Anderson's "Money in the Bank," Reba McEntire's "The Heart is a Lonely Hunter," George Strait's "Blue Clear Sky," Jo Dee Messina's "Heads Carolina, Tails California," Lonestar's "No News," Ricochet's "Daddy's Money" and Trace Adkins's "This Ain't No Thinkin' Thing." More than ten of them climbed all the way to number one. In 1997, ASCAP named Mark their Songwriter of the Year, and the song "No News" was named Song of

the Year. His catalogue of songs helped MCA Music win the Publisher of the Year award, as well.

There are so many other great songwriters in this town that it's hard to talk about them all. In recent years, Tom Shapiro, Bob DePiero, Kostas, Hugh Prestwood, Mike Reid, Dave Loggins, Gary Burr, Don Von Tress, John Ims and several others have won major awards from either BMI or ASCAP acknowledging the success of the songs they've written, and have made a big difference in the careers of several artists. Those songs include "Wink," by Neal McCoy; "She's in Love With the Boy," by Trisha Yearwood;

"Lost in the Fifties Tonight" and "Stranger in My House," for Ronnie Milsap; "Achy Breaky Heart," by Billy Ray Cyrus; "She Is His Only Love," by Wynonna; Dwight Yoakam's "Ain't That Lonely Yet" and "What Mattered Most," by Ty Herndon.

Among others who have made major inroads into the business is Beth Nielsen Chapman, who, starting in the late 1980s, has been involved in writing a string of hits including Tanya Tucker's "Strong Enough To Bend," Willie Nelson's "Nothing I Can Do About It Now" and Faith Hill's "This Kiss," which she wrote with two other women, Annie Roboff and Robin Lerner. Beth's also had some very successful albums of her own along the way.

Craig Wiseman introduced us to "Bubba Hyde" in a very funny hit for Diamond Rio, as well as writing "If the Good Die Young" for Tracy Lawrence and "Where the Green Grass Grows" for Tim McGraw.

And the list goes on and on.

Every night in Nashville, at the Bluebird Cafe and Douglas Corner, in the clubs along Lower Broadway and in Printer's Alley and in hotels and listening rooms all around town, there are songwriters showing off their new material. Each one hopes they've written the song that will change his or her life—the one that will be heard by millions of listeners around the world. Publishing companies regularly are on the lookout for the next Harlan Howard or Roger Miller to nurture into a profitable hit maker. Each year, a few more make it to the top for the first time, giving hope to all the others who just keep plugging away, waiting for their turn, because they know it all begins with a song.

The Musicians

Though Nashville was rapidly attracting many tal-

Left to right: Songwriters Bob DePiero and Tom Shapiro stand proudly on the stage with BMI's Francis Preston after their song "Wink" is named Song of the Year (1995); Master songwriter and producer Norro Wilson stands next to an old poster from his days as a singer (1999); Jimmy Webb, writer of songs like "Wichita Lineman" and "MacArthur Park", sings at a songwriter's conference (1991); Songwriters Matraca Berg and Gary Harrison proudly display their CMA Song of the Year awards for "Strawberry Wine" (1997).

ented musicians, it still didn't have its own commercial recording studio until the late '40s. Talented musicians had to go to other cities to record with Nashville's country stars. Harold Bradley traveled to Chicago in 1946 to record with P. W. King, and Owen Bradley went there to record with Eddy Arnold.

In 1947, Castle Recording Studio opened in Nashville. Ironically, the first work the Bradleys did there wasn't for a hit song; instead, it was a jingle for a local jeweler named Harold L. Shires. On the session were Harold Bradley on guitar, Owen Bradley on piano, Farris Coursey on drums, George Cooper on bass, and Snooky Lanson, who became nationally famous for singing vocals on the 1950s television show *Your Hit Parade*.

Later that year, Decca Records executive Paul Cohen became the first record producer to come to record sessions in Nashville, because he realized it was cheaper than paying room and board for artists and musicians to stay in Cincinnati or New York to record for a month. That was the beginning of Nashville's recording industry. The first cut for Red Foley featured Owen Bradley on organ and so impressed the executives in New York that they asked for his tracks to be re-recorded a little louder. The song, "Tennessee Border," rose to number three on the *Billboard* charts in 1949.

Harold Bradley called the early group of musicians the "pioneers." Drummer Farris Coursey is probably best known for slapping his thigh black and blue during Red Foley's "Chattanoogie Shoe Shine

Boy," which stayed at number one on the country charts for thirteen weeks in 1950. Grady Martin played lead guitar on that song and many others. In the 1970s, Willie Nelson brought Grady out of session work and into his band many years after Grady thought he'd quit the road.

Others among the pioneers who played at Castle include Ernie Newton playing bass, Jack Shook on rhythm guitar and tenor banjo, and Bob Foster or Don Davis on steel guitar. Don Helms, who played with Hank Williams, did some session work there, as did Hank Garland and Bob Moore. Many of the tracks recorded there featured Tommy Jackson on the fiddle, and Marty Hughes often played piano when Owen was otherwise involved. Harold Bradley played lead, rhythm and electric guitar and whatever else was necessary to create a hit.

The Bradleys opened their first studio in 1951,

Clockwise from top left: Danny Davis reads the music trade magazines as he rides on the bus to his next destination (1985); Legendary "A-Team" drummer, Buddy Harmon, performs behind artists at Fanfair (1978); Grady Martin, a session player included among The Pioneers and the A-Team, plays with Willie Nelson at Farmaid VI (1993).

the second one in Nashville, at Second and Lindsley above a lodge hall, until the owner tripled the rent. From there, they moved to a studio in Hillsboro Village for a few years. When Paul Cohen suggested moving the recording sessions to Dallas, Owen and Harold didn't want to move, so they bought a house on 16th Avenue for $7500 and built the first studio on what would become Music Row. They hired a builder named Joe Crane to attach a prefabricated building behind it. The new studio's name, the Quonset Hut, came from the surplus army materials from which it was made.

As the music business changed, many of the pioneers retired or were replaced as newer musicians were attracted to Nashville. Many overlapped the transition, like Harold Bradley, Grady Martin, Buddy Emmons, Otto Bash and Bob Moore. Drummer

Buddy Harman and guitarist Ray Edenton soon became regulars in the ever changing Nashville music business. The more versatile you were with music and musical instruments, the more work you could get. Charlie McCoy, best known for his abilities with the harmonica, played everything, thus creating a niche for a category known as "utility player." This was a time when many incredible musicians heard the siren call and came to Nashville.

When I moved here, I began to hear the term *The A Team*, which was used to describe the best players in Nashville. This group of players consisted of Hank Garland, Ray Edenton, Grady Martin and Harold Bradley as the guitarists. Bob Moore played bass and Buddy Harman played drums. It also included Charlie McCoy, Boots Randolph on saxophone, Tommy Jackson on fiddle, Pete Drake on steel and Floyd Cramer and Hargus "Pig" Robbins on keyboard.

In the 1960s and '70s, Jerry Carrigan, David Briggs, Norbert Putnam, Reggie Young and others soon migrated up here from the Muscle Shoals,

Alabama, recording scene. Several studio players, like Boots Randolph and Danny Davis, whose group, Danny Davis and the Nashville Brass, won the CMA's Musician of the Year award from 1969 to 1974, had very successful recording careers in their own right.

Musicians like Wayne Moss and Jim Covard, who were part of Barefoot Jerry, also did lots session work, as did Charlie Daniels and Jerry Reed, both of whom eventually won CMA Musician of the Year awards. Other CMA winners over the years have included Chet Atkins, Charlie McCoy, Don Rich, Johnny Gimble, Roy Clark, my personal favorite, Hargus "Pig" Robbins. During this time, the word continued to spread, and other great musicians began coming from everywhere, including Memphis, Detroit, New York and Los Angeles, realizing that they could make a good living in Nashville.

At one of the first sessions I photographed, I observed as a new songwriter tried to explain to the musicians how he thought the song should sound. After several false starts, he said, "Can you make it sound a little more like Jerry Lee Lewis?" The piano player, responded, "You mean like this?" and proceeded to take the song into rockabilly. The other musicians joined in quickly, and the tracks for the song were completed in no time. Since then, I've seen this happen many times.

Several of the greatest players I've photographed since the 1980s I first photographed playing at the Station Inn, the home of Nashville's bluegrass scene.

They include Mark O'Connor, Jerry Douglas, Sam Bush, Stuart Duncan, Randy Howard, Bela Fleck and double bass virtuoso, Edgar Meyer. Since then, these gifted musicians have been regularly featured in sessions and onstage, performing many styles of music. Mark O'Connor, who won the CMA Musician of the Year from 1991 to 1996, and Edgar Meyer have gained fame in the classical music world on their own, especially for their album with renowned cellist Yo-Yo Ma in 1996. After leaving New Grass Revival, Bela Fleck moved into the field of jazz with his group, the Flecktones, winning Grammys along the way. His recent album reunites him with some of those players for a return to his bluegrass roots.

For the past eleven years, *Music Row* magazine has named the top studio musicians based on their work on albums that make it into the Top Ten on *Billboard*'s country charts. The 1999 winners included CMA award winner Brent Mason, who played guitar on twenty-three of the top fifty albums. Steven J. Nathan matched that record on keyboards, and Stuart Duncan performed fiddle on twenty of the albums. Drummers Paul Leim and Eddie Bayers tied at fourteen albums each.

Glen Worf, who was a member of the Kingsnakes in the 1980s and now is in the Bluebloods, found time to use his bass-playing skills on seventeen top ten albums, winning for the eighth year in a row. Veteran singer and songwriter John Wesley Ryles received honors for his work as a back-

This page: Charlie McCoy, one of the best sessions players, who plays more than just an harmonica, inspires an audience at The Exit In (1975); facing page, top to bottom: Between the two of them, most of the sessions from 1946 into the 1980's involved Chet Atkins or Harold Bradley as the guitarist (1991); When Tanya Tucker realized Hargus "Pig" Robbins was the piano player who'd been playing on her sessions since she was a teenager, she plopped into his lap to give him a big hug (1996).

Left to right: The late, great Roy Husky, Jr., waits his turn to play bass on the stage of the Grand Ole Opry (1994); Legendary Muscle Shoals musician, Reggie Young, works on yet a another session in Nashville (1998); David Schnaufer, the world's greatest dulcimer player, sits on my front porch for a photo to be used for his first album cover (1986); Mark Casstevens, who played at Opryland when I worked there in 1973, performs on a session for Tracey Lawrence (1997).

ground vocalist on eighteen albums. The incredible steel guitar player Paul Franklin beat them all by contributing his talents to an astonishing twenty-eight of the top charting albums.

Though these guys are the current winners, they are only the tip of Nashville's musical iceberg. Other great musicians working at the time of this writing include Brent Rowan, Steve Gibson, Mark Casstevens, Biff Watson, Larry Byrom and Chris Leuzinger on guitar. Among the successful bass players are Michael Rhodes, Mike Brignardello and Mike Chapman. Fiddle players Larry Franklin and Aubrey Haynie have stayed very busy doing session work, as

has Lonnie Wilson on drums. Liana Manis, Dennis Wilson and Curtis Young, who had won several previous awards as a background singer, lent their voices to more than ten albums each.

Steel guitarists include Sonny Garrish, Dan Dugmore and Bruce Bouton. Keyboard players John Hobbs, Matt Rollings and John Barlow Jarvis also have stayed very busy. Vince Gill, Steve Wariner, Sammy Kershaw and Alan Jackson have depended on Hargus "Pig" Robbins to play piano on some of their albums. Other personal favorites of mine include Terry McMillan on harmonica and David Schnaufer on dulcimer.

It's no wonder that the Nashville studio musicians passed up New York for recording sessions in the mid-1990s, doubling their payroll from six to twelve million dollars. They also exceed the players in Los Angeles for sessions in the record industry, though Los Angeles still dominates the film and television recordings. But with so many Nashville songs being used in those industries, I don't think it will be long before we close that gap as well.

While the Lovin' Spoonful's 1966 classic song "Nashville Cats" exaggerated the number of "guitar pickers" in Nashville, even then, they weren't wrong to be amazed at all the musicians in Music City.

The 1998 American Federation of Musicians Nashville membership book lists over 1700 guitarists, 700 keyboard players, 500 drummers, and 250 banjo players. From accordions to bagpipes, kazoos to zithers, Nashville has someone who can play virtually any instrument in existence, and some who invent and play their own like Futureman, a member of the Flecktones, and the incredible Junior Brown. I continue to be excited when I get to cover a recording session, wondering what magic I'll get to hear next.

The Nashville Symphony and the Blair School of Music have brought classical music to the forefront for many years. The music union fronted the re-starting of the symphony in 1946 with 1,000 dollars, at a time when that was a lot of money to a membership that was only four years old. Many artists like Amy Grant, Vince Gill, Michael Martin Murphy, Gary Morris and Roger Miller have performed with them since then, showing just how small the crossroads of the music community are in this town.

Today, the community also supports the W. O. Smith School of Music, where many of our top musicians take time to give lessons to children who would otherwise never have the chance to enter the world of music. Harold Bradley refers to Nashville as "the last oasis for free enterprise music" in the country. Judging by the statistics, this musical watering hole is only going to get bigger in years to come. I look forward to my next chance to see its stars at work.

Videos—Three Minute Movies

Since the 1980's, when music videos began to come into fashion, Nashville has become quite a little movie town. A number of production companies, studios and editing facilities have sprung up since then, and many budding producers, directors, writers, cinematographers and technicians have moved here to make a living. The result has been hundreds of videos, many of which have won awards and helped establish the careers of many artists working in Nashville.

My first experience on a video shoot still ranks as the funniest. As Nashville began to experiment at Culture Club was much more complicated than anyone thought.

The first difficulty was getting those guys to wear makeup and dresses. There was definitely some hesitation on the part of these two men with someone thinking of them differently after seeing the video. Makeup artist Vanessa Sellers and costumer Valerie Wise took great pains at transforming the guys, constantly reassuring them that there wouldn't be a problem. Still, Moe held out until Joe was completely in costume. He still doesn't like to talk about it, but once he got into character, he was great.

One of the scenes involved a mock setup of the Grand Ole Opry and a guest appearance by Roy Acuff. The boys were in complete drag outfits when Roy arrived, and they were understandably nervous about his reaction. When he saw them, he just cracked up with laughter, and said, "Well, boys, if it makes you money." I found out many years later that when he was entering his performing career and worked with a traveling "Snake Oil" salesman, he often had to wear costumes that included pretending to be an Indian and a pigtail girl in a gingham dress. He understood and did his part well to help them with their project.

Since then, I've seen many singers have to learn how to act and trust the video crews to make them look like they knew what they were doing. I've also seen many who understood completely. Here is a gallery of those who have learned, on the job, how to be actors as well as singers.

Makeup artist, Vanessa Sellars, poses with her art work, Moe Bandy and Joe Stampley, in drag for the video of "Where's the Dress" (1984).

Clockwise from top left: Tim McGraw works on the video for "Sleep on It Tonight" (1996); Holly Dunn gets roped by a cowboy during her video shoot (1995); Dolly Parton causes Ricky Van Shelton to melt when she touches his cheek on the set for the video of "Rockin' Chair" (1991); Mark Chesnutt gets the giggles on a take for his video (1996).

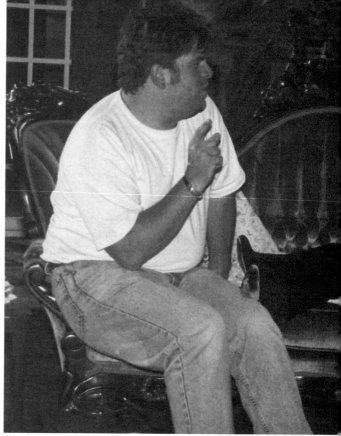

Clockwise from top left: Vern Gosdin sings his heart out at the Loveless Motel for the video of "That Just About Does It" (1989); Award-winning director, Steve Goldmann, talks with Shelby Lynne about her video shot in her home town, Mobile, Alabama (1995); Joe Diffie sings through a kitchen window for the video of "Is It Cold In Here" (1991); John Anderson makes a cameo appearance on Run C& W's only video (1992); First Avenue South in Nashville is turned into deep winter in Russia for the video of "Famine" recorded by the Gospel group, The Nelons (1986); Billy Ray Cyrus works on a video for a NASCAR racing album (1995); Randy Travis sings on the set of the video for "Forever and Ever, Amen" (1987).

Shel SILVERSTEIN

Left to right: Bobby Bare and Shel Silverstein stop for a moment after finishing their album Lullabies, Legends and Lies (1974); Shel Silverstein joins Dr. Hook & the Medicine Show on stage at The Exit In (1975).

Shel Silverstein could be called a modern renaissance man. I first paid attention to his work in Playboy, where he was one of the cartoonists who filled the spaces between the naked ladies and the advertising. I loved his offbeat humor. Later, he would be sent out on junkets, where he would report on the Bohemian lifestyles he viewed around the world, complete with sketches.

Then, as I am told, he and fellow Playboy cartoonist, Herb Gardner, talked about what else they wanted to do. Herb wanted to write plays and movies; Shel wanted to write songs and poems. Both of them succeeded beyond their wildest dreams. Herb's many plays and movies, like *A Thousand Clowns* and *I'm Not Rappaport*, have brought him great success.

Shel's songs, like "The Hills of Shiloh" and "The Unicorn," from the folk era; Dr. Hook & the Medicine Show's "Cover of the Rolling Stone" and "Freakin' at the Freaker's Ball"; Johnny Cash's "A Boy Named Sue"; Bobby Bare's "Marie Laveau" and "Daddy What If"; Loretta Lynn's "Hey Loretta"; and the Old Dogs project on Atlantic Records, with Mel Tillis, Waylon Jennings, Bobby Bare and Jerry Reed, show how well he did at songwriting. Add to that his Grammy award-winning children's album and inspiring children's books, like *The Giving Tree* and *Where the Sidewalk Ends*, and you know how well he did with his dreams. He shall be missed, but never forgotten.

7 | GARTH BROOKS

This page, top to bottom: Garth makes his first Fanfair appearance on the Songwriter's Show shortly before landing a record deal (1988); Sandy and Garth celebrate his #1 single at one of many ASCAP parties to come (1990); facing page: Garth is moved by the reaction from Nashville Now!'s audience after he sings "If Tomorrow Never Comes" (1990).

G B, the Garthman, the G-man, the Garth Monster or just plain Garth Brooks. It is hard to explain this man who jumped on the pickup truck we call country music. It was as if he climbed into the cab, fiddled with the stick shift and found a gear no one had noticed. The truck suddenly leaped into the air and took off. Not even the truck knew it was capable of going this far. Garth did.

A lot of people have made Garth a punching bag since his success. I have to admit up front to an obvious prejudice in favor of Garth and his wife, Sandy, and their families. They come from strong working-class backgrounds. They come from families who believe in the American Dream. I consider them friends.

When I met them, they were still settling into Nashville, not too long after they quit selling boots in Goodletsville. Actually, I had met Garth in 1988, in Bob Doyle's office shortly after Bob left his secure job at ASCAP to become a publisher with two signed writers, Buddy Mundlock from Chicago, and Garth Brooks from Stillwater, Oklahoma.

Garth was among a group of writers who sang on Fanfair 1988's *NSAI Songwriters Show* along with Paul Overstreet, Kevin Welch and several others. Those shots were MIF, missing in file, for several years when I decided to look through outtakes I had kept. I'd forgotten he was one of the performers.

Major Robert Doyle, former member of the

Tennessee Air National Guard, had decided to become a publisher, naming his company Major Bob Music. At the same time, my friend Pam Lewis was busting her butt to run a freelance life as a publicist. A twenty-six-year-old whiz kid from MTV, she left New York for RCA Records in Nashville. Disagreements with label executives caused her to leave not too long after her arrival. Her involvement in promoting Bob's acts soon led to the management team that brought Garth Brooks to the forefront.

On his first trip to Nashville, Garth was told to go home and think about it. He did. The constructive criticism did not stop his dream—it only gave him more desire to succeed in the music business. As I have learned in my own life, sometimes those who tell you that you are not capable of doing something are the ones that make you so determined that you cannot help but succeed.

When I first met Garth and Sandy, they had just gone through the hardest part of their lives, settling into a new community and learning about the pitfalls of the music business. I found them worrying about their gamble, but believing in their future. I found them real and very special people.

I don't think they ever dreamed just how big they could become. Handling the horse called music when it gallops out of control has killed many a performer and far too many marriages. Somehow, they have survived it, growing through it as real as they possibly could.

Garth is one of the most hands-on artists I've ever seen. I have seen him load the bus, carry the mike

This page: George Jones praises the man and his accomplishments from the Fanfair stage as Garth tries to choke back his emotions (1991); facing page: Garth sings to a small crowd at Country Radio Seminar about the time his first single is released (1989).

stands, and hang from the rafters setting lights. His desire to see it done well leads him to know every aspect of his job. Sometimes, in trying to do his best, he's gotten his fingers burned. Welcome to the music business. God bless the artist who tries to keep the keys to his car.

1989 brought him his first album and a single called "Much Too Young to Feel This Damn Old." He sang at *Country Radio Seminar* for United Stations Radio Network in front of a sparse crowd as the syndicating network tried to get a live music show started as a drawing card for their suite. It was here that he met Victoria Shaw, which led to their co-writing of "The River." It was here that he met radio.

I honestly don't remember hearing him that night. I was too busy covering the madness that comes with sticking several hundred radio people in the Opryland Hotel's Presidential Suite. The next day, I stopped by Pam Lewis's office to show her my pictures and she gave me a pre-release tape of his album. I listened to it in my truck while going home and was blown away. Every cut was worth hearing again. And he had picked Allen Reynolds, one of my favorite producers, who was instrumental in the careers of Don Williams, Crystal Gayle and Kathy Mattea. I called Pam and asked her to keep me in mind when it was time for more photos. I had a hunch about this kid.

Soon after, at a Capitol Records party, I met Sandy and was totally charmed. I understood why Garth was crawling back to her after he had fallen for the seductions of the road. When I asked him what he wanted to me to photograph, he said, "You take as many pictures of Sandy and me as you possibly can." I was happy to comply.

"Much Too Young" peaked at number eight but made an impact with the critics and his number of fans were multiplying. His appearance at Fanfair 1989 showed a small, but growing interest in this new artist. Garth began plowing a path on the road that would not stop for three years.

In October, Garth showcased at Talent Buyers, a convention that brought the performers, the booking agents and those looking for acts to fill their facilities. Garth shook hands and charmed them in his show-case. There was a buzz about him everywhere you went. The owner of Toolie's in Arizona said he'd already booked him for the following year, saying he wouldn't be playing clubs that size for much longer. He was right.

A number of the staff and family members were there, as were Sandy and Garth. I was talking to them when Tanya came into the room. She saw Garth and started singing his new single, "If Tomorrow Never Comes", to him. He was embarrassed but took it in stride. Then she smacked him on the cheek and went over to talk to someone else. I laughed and told him I'd just taken her picture kissing Clint just fifteen minutes before. "Damn", he said with a chuckle," that kid's always fifteen minutes ahead of me." The new single went number one exactly two months later. The following year, Garth took the Horizon trophy home with him, and has never looked back.

The ball was rolling in 1990. This time when Garth sang in the Presidential Suite at Country Radio Seminar, the room was packed. March also brought him his second #1, "Not Counting You", and he took time off to celebrate at ASCAP along with co-writer Kent Blazey, taking just a moment off from his grueling road schedule. Two weeks later, on St. Patrick's Day, he and Kent picked up their first award from NSAI for "If Tomorrow Never Comes". They named it Song of the Year.

In May, I shot the CEMA distributors convention, and although he wasn't there, everyone was talking about him. When the people who put the records in the stores are excited about someone, you know their music is getting on the shelves. Garth, of course, was

This page: Garth spends the day signing autographs and greeting fans in his Fanfair booth (1992); facing page: When Garth is surprised with his first Gold Album, he walks out to the edge of the stage to share it with the people who helped him get it (1990).

somewhere on the road singing for his growing legion of fans, the ones who would be buying the records.

Along with the heat and humidity, June brought Nashville another Fanfair. This year, Garth's reception was different. Crowds poured into the line that took them in front of the stage. Rousing ovations greeted every song. Suddenly, the flow was interrupted by Jimmy Bowen, head of Capitol Records, who wanted to say something about Garth's success. He surprised Garth and Sandy with a gold record for the first album. Garth was overwhelmed. He thanked his family and everyone else he could think of, then walked out beyond the mike to hold the album up to the fans who had made this possible. No other gold albums were marked after that. All of the sales recognition's after that started with platinum.

Later in June, Garth worked on a video version of the song that would be the first single of the next album. I stopped by to cover the filming and had a blast. Sandy greeted me by showing me her biker tattoo, Garth posed for photos with "a few of his fans"

and Little Jimmy Dickens made a cameo appearance looking taller than he ever had. The song was "Friends in Low Places". I loved it.

During a break, he stopped to do a few video spots, including one for some friends who were getting married. He couldn't make it to their wedding, so he made this as a surprise.

At the number one party in April, I had given he and Sandy a copy of the first photo I'd taken of them together, with a note I'd scribbled on the back. As he made his apologies for not being there, he quoted what I had written. "May your love last longer than the music." I was stunned. What a memory he had!

During this taping, I shot a few silhouettes of him as the lights came up. The next day while the band was loading up for the road, I stopped by and delivered contact sheets. Garth and crew were loading the bus, so I shot a few shots of that. June also brought a #1 party for Tony Arata's heart tugging song "The Dance". The first time I saw the video, I cried. I still get choked up by that song. It won Video of the Year at the CMA Awards in 1990.

In August, when I knew GB would be in the office, I took the Fanfair gold record shot by the Doyle/Lewis office to get it autographed. As an afterthought, I took along my favorite silhouette shot to show them. Garth loved it. He began saying he wanted it on the back of his upcoming album. Bob and Pam kept saying it was too late. Garth was insistent. He called Virginia Team, the art director, who was

A father holds his child up so he can shake Garth's hand (1992).

This page: The writers of "Friends in Low Places", Earl Bud Lee and Dewayne Blackwell, celebrate their #1 record with Garth Brooks (1990); facing page: Sandy proudly holds Garth's CMA Horizon Award as he thanks everyone, especially her (1990).

completing the project.

He began by saying," Virginia, there's nothing I can do to make you mad, is there?" There was a pause. "I have a new idea for the back of the cover." There was a long pause. "Well, can I at least bring it down and show it to you?" He and Bob and Pam and I crowded into Bob's old pickup truck and drove the few blocks to Virginia's office.

It was obvious that we were too late. The final artwork was sitting there ready and approved. Still, Garth tried to make a case for changing it. He suggested layout changes, but Virginia kept pointing out it was ready to go to the presses. Jimmy Bowen's assistant came over from Capitol with the facts and figures on how much it would cost and how long it would delay the album release. Garth gave in, then turned to me and apologized, saying," Don't worry,

we'll use it somewhere." It became an office logo, was used on a T-shirt and tour book and as a thank you in the trade magazines. It remains one of my favorite shots.

Fall of 1990, the Garth rocket took off. "Friends in Low Places" shot up the charts in seven weeks, and the album, "No Fences", quickly took the top spot on the country charts and stayed there forever. I saw co-writer Bud Lee in Rio Bravo during that time and he was worried about how fast it was rising. He figured it would flash and die before his eyes. I predicted it would be out there for a long time, especially on juke-boxes in every honeytonk in the world. I was right. It stayed number one in Billboard for five weeks.

October brought him the CMA Horizon Award and more surprises. Two days after the award, he and his mother, a Capitol Records artist for a short while before he was born, donated items to The Country Music Hall of Fame, then went up the street to Capitol for an expected award for the first album going platinum. By the time the event was planned, No Fences, too, had gone platinum. 1990 closed with "Unanswered Prayers", co-written with Pat Alger and Larry Bastian at #1 in Radio & Record for four weeks and 3 weeks in Billboard. Garth was becoming a phe-nomenon. Still, he was digging deep ruts in the road as he criss-crossed America singing his songs for as many people as possible.

1991 brought a number one for Garth, Dennis Robbins and Bobby Boyd, as writers of the song "Two of a Kind" in March, and controversy for his

next song "The Thunder Rolls" in June. The first time I heard this song, Trisha Yearwood sang it at Douglas Corner with Pat Alger's Algerian Trio, complete with the final verse which did not make the album. I was floored by the song, and the vocalist, as well. But that's another chapter.

"The Thunder Rolls" spent three weeks on the charts at #1, but the video which included the final verse, was banned from TNN and CMT. The truth it spoke about violence in the home was way beyond their capacity to underwrite. Though they may have understood it, they chose to avoid the subject, worried that it would only make matters worse. In the

fall, the CMA members gave it their award for Video of the Year. Director, Bud Schaetzle, as he accepted the award, thanked CMT and TNN for their help in bringing the video to everyone's attention.

Two weeks before the awards show, Capitol released "Ropin' the Wind". It broke all records by entering the Billboard charts at #1. No other country act in history had done this. Garth was surprised in his sweats at CMA headquarters by hundreds of friends and supporters. They included a new duo called Brooks and Dunn.

Backstage at the CMA's that year were insane, with the usual chaos complicated by a visit from George and Barbara Bush. Secret Service was everywhere, and a metal detector was set up just outside Roy Acuff's dressing room. While the motorcade with the President was winding its way up Briley Parkway from the airport, I was back by the artist's busses watching Garth and his band members tossing a football in the parking lot.

He was in his sweats, and still hadn't shaved for the show, when Pam Lewis came out with all the EMI/Capitol executives to meet him. Then she informed him that President Bush had requested his prescience at a reception before the show.

Garth went to the bus, made a quick change into a tux and we all started toward the Opryhouse. As we walked across the parking lot, the Presidential motorcade, complete with a black helicopter hovering overhead, made its way to The Opryland Hotel. At the same time, the limo with Sandy and his parents came up to the backstage entrance.

All traffic stopped, leaving the Brooks family sitting outside a locked gate. Garth became worried about not connecting with his family, and wouldn't leave until he knew they would. Mickey, his road manager, stayed behind to take care of them while we went into the backstage area. They joined us a short time later.

I followed Sandy and Garth through the metal detector only to be told it would be another 30 minutes before the Bushes would be there. They went back to his dressing room. He changed tuxes and waited. Finally, when the time came, we went back through the metal detectors to a secured area where several other artists stood on risers waiting for a Presidential photo-op. I was ushered to a platform directly across from them where all the music business photographers and TV crews were waiting. The Washington Press Corps had their own platform, separate from us.

When the Bushes arrived, they talked to George Jones, Barbara Mandrell and a few others then joined the rest of the artists on the platforms. They stood directly in front of Garth and Sandy, and never said a word to them. Later, when Garth received his Entertainer award, he said, "I would like to thank my two George's, George Jones and George Strait. No offense, Mr. President." I was six rows behind Mr. Bush and could see several Secret Service agents in the room look at the President to see his reaction. When he laughed, they laughed, too. So did I.

Confession is good for the soul, so they say, so maybe now is the time to come clean. I did not vote for Garth as entertainer that year because I thought he needed a little more seasoning. But I had never been to one of his shows. I had never seen the Garth Monster do a full show for 22,000 hard core believers.

When I was in college and shooting Austin Peay State University's NCAA bound basketball team during their championship years in the 1970's, I got to hear crowds scream so loud, you couldn't hear the buzzer at half-time. Some of those games were in

This page: President George Bush addresses the CMA audience (1991); facing page: Garth is overjoyed by the phenomenal success of his album, Ropin' The Wind, after it enters the Billboard Top Album charts at #1, a first for a country album (1991).

newly constructed Murphy Center at Middle Tennessee State University. I heard that sound again November 7th, 1991.

I arrived in the afternoon and watched some setup and rehearsal. Garth was above the stage goofing with the lights, then climbing down one of those ladders you see circus acrobats using under the big top. He went up to the back of the room, in the cheap seats and looked at the stage, trying to see what they would see.

Meanwhile, Bud Schaetzle's High Five film crews were finishing up some filler scenes for Garth's first TV special, so the place was turning into a monstrous video shoot. Cables and camera tracks were everywhere. I shot a few more backstage shots and headed for the area directly in front of the stage.

As I walked up the ramp into Murphy Center, I heard that sound I remembered from the basketball tournaments. The room was on fire. 22,000 people stood around the arena waiting for Garth. Someone started the wave as I stood in front of the stage, and I turned to follow them full circle. No other concert I've seen before or since had such electricity, except for other Garth concerts.

I soon learned that shooting a Garth concert was like shooting a basketball game. He went around the stage like a player at full court press. I learned to let him come to me rather than try to chase him. Even that was difficult to do, because from concert to concert, I found no planned pattern. He would cover the

THIS WEEK	LAST WEEK	2 WKS AGO	WKS. ON CHART	ARTIST	TITLE	PEAK POSITION
1	NEW	1		**GARTH BROOKS** CAPITOL NASHVILLE	**ROPIN' THE WIND**	1
2	1	1	5	META ELEKTRA	METALLICA	1
3	2	2	14	NA LE ELEKTRA	UNFORGETTABLE	1
4	5	4	8	CO BADD GIANT	C.M.B.	3
5	4	3	12	BO TT CAPITOL	LUCK OF THE DRAW	2
6	6	5	18	BO MOTOWN	COOLEYHIGHHARMONY	3
7	10			FACTORY COLUMBIA	GONNA MAKE YOU SWEAT	2
8				TON COLUMBIA	TIME, LOVE AND TENDERNESS	1
9				OS.	OUT OF TIME	1
					ROLL THE BONES	3

THE Billboard 200 TOP ALBUMS FOR WEEK ENDING SEPTEMBER 28, 1991

whole stage, sing to every part of his audience, but never entirely the same from show to show. It was like watching a tiger in a cage.

I knew I'd made a mistake in my vote for Entertainer of the Year. Never have I seen so much energy expended for the sake of a country music audience. John Cougar Mellencamp's opening act performance before Heart at Municipal Auditorium in 1983 would be considered by me, but he's not considered country. Pearl Jam was loud and interesting, but lacked focus. It's hard to beat GB when it comes to igniting an audience.

I was so blown away by the Murfreesboro concert that I immediately signed up for his concert in Charlotte, North Carolina. December 14th would be the final show in what became known as the "Garth Brooks, No Fences, Ropin' the Wind" tour. The G-man had toured for three years solid, and would finally take a break.

One of the funniest stage pranks I've ever seen occurred during the Charlotte show. A few weeks before in Atlanta one of the stagehands brought a can of "Silly-String" on stage during the "Friends in Low Places" segment and surprised Garth by spraying him with it. Garth loved it so much, he suggested that they keep it in. For the finale show, his brother, Kelly bought a whole case of the stuff and passed it out to everyone he could find. When the moment came, people came from everywhere spraying him until every bit of it was gone. Garth looked like a caterpillar in a cocoon when they were finished. The audi-

ence loved it and the band kept vamping as he tried to stop laughing and peel himself out of his multi-colored shell.

Backstage after the show, his staff and friends surprised him with a wrap party. He was moved by this show of support as they toasted his success. Then he toasted them, thanking them for their help, and finished by saying,"...but remember, the star that burns brightest, burns out quickest." It was a chilling remark that showed he aware that sustaining a career was just as hard as getting one started. He knew that 1992 wasn't going to be any easier than the rigorous journey he had made as he scrambled to the top.

The new year brought the news that Sandy and Garth were going to be parents. Family and friends were elated. The public interest in the new superstar couple was bubbling, and security worries began growing. Still, Garth was reluctant to see himself in such a light. This year would change all that.

The new year also brought Garth's first TV special. Aired on NBC, it came in ninth in viewership that week and put everyone on notice that he was more than just a country star. He attracted an audience that would have been the envy of an rock or pop star in the world. With all the new eyes and ears that tuned in, all of Garth's albums began selling like hotcakes. Nashville had never seen anything like it. Soon, the other labels were looking for artists that could take advantage of this potential. Veterans like Ken Kragen, who had guided the careers of artists like Kenny Rogers and was the driving force behind "We

Are The World", wisely warned the industry against trotting out Garth clones.

Country Radio Seminar came back around in March and the unknown guy from 1989 was in demand. He did the Superfaces show for the radio folks and tons of interviews, as well as, the Grand Old Opry while he was in town. Then, in April, near tragedy struck.

As Garth and Sandy traveled to the American Music Awards in California, Sandy, tired from her pregnancy and busy life, collapsed in the Los Angeles airport. It turned out to be nothing more than dehydration and exhaustion, but it was a wake up call to Garth. He couldn't just think of career anymore, he was about to be a father, and that created a crisis he had not expected.

A lot of cynics saw this conflict as a publicity stunt, but they didn't see Garth's hair turn gray almost overnight. I had seen him shortly before Sandy's collapse and a few weeks after. He was truly changed by this near tragedy. He realized he had to learn how to balance family and career, something every bread-winner discovers before he knows how to handle the conflict. Despite his ever increasing fame, he was no different than any other expectant father.

Despite Sandy's delicate condition, Garth continued to be a busy man. The Academy of Country Music named him Entertainer of the Year for 1992,

and his albums were selling at an unheard of pace not just for country, but for all categories. His first TV special taped in 1991 played twice on NBC and did very well in the ratings. His singles from Ropin' the Wind were also climbing to the top of the radio airplay charts. After a few months off, he resumed touring, while keeping an ever watchful eye toward home.

He and Sandy had just bought a beautiful house on a hill in Goodletsville, a suburb of Nashville. While it was being customized for them, they lived in a double-wide trailer there on the property. Security was beginning to be a problem with his ever increasing fame. Though he had tried hard not to take himself that seriously, with a family on the way, things sadly had to change. After a couple of people were caught on the property, Garth relented and allowed guards to be posted 24 hours a day.

But Garth didn't let all of these new found problems stop him from entertaining his fans. He gave one of his finest performances at Fanfair that June. He'd had a few months to rest and get in shape, and when he hit the stage, he was as eager and happy as the audience. Then he spent hours meeting the fans at his booth. He truly was enjoying himself getting to meet them. But some of them weren't fans.

With the birth of his first child just weeks away, a woman walked up and asked Garth to hold a baby

This page: Garth is covered in "Silly String" by everyone, including Trisha Yearwood, during the final show of a marathon three year tour (1991); Facing page: This time, Garth chooses to climb a ladder to get closer to his audience (1993); inset: Music City finally gets to see a Garth Brooks concert after it opens The Nashville Arena (1998);

so she could take a photo. He suggested she be in the picture, as well, but she wouldn't. He held the baby out away from himself, suspecting something. Sure enough, after Taylor was born, it showed up on the cover of a magazine with a headline telling the world Garth and Sandy were raising their child in a trailer. Then someone followed them all the way back to Oklahoma hoping to get a photo of the real Taylor Mayne Pearl Brooks. There were rumors that some-one was offering $100,000 for that photo. I can honestly say that this was an exaggeration of what would really be paid.

With Taylor born and the household secure, Garth turned his attention to Christmas. He had just finished Beyond the Season, his first album of Christmas songs, and had talked his label into donating one dollar per album sold that year to Feed the Children. Though it was only August, he wanted to get an early start.

To promote the album and the charity, Garth went on a whirlwind tour of the United States, hitting seven cities across the United States in three days. I was lucky enough to be chosen to go on this marathon.

Everyone connected in Texas for the first press/fan conference at Billy Bob's in Ft. Worth. In keeping with the theme of the album, the club was decked out in Christmas decorations and Santa made an early visit to support the cause. Larry Jones, whose charitable orga-nization was the beneficiary of this unique fund-raiser, was ecstatic at the turnout. He spoke in glowing terms of how good album sales would help him get food and other supplies to children who were in need of help.

This page: Garth and Sandy wait backstage before the CMA Awards Show (1991). facing page: Garth performs "Friends in Low Places" at a Talent Buyers convention long before the single is released (1989).

Garth answered questions from press and fans alike. After a successful time in Texas, we headed for the air-port to catch a ride to California. As we flew across the country, hurricane Andrew was bearing down on Florida. Within hours, that impending disaster would have a direct bearing on what we were doing. By the time we got to Berkley, the storm was grinding its way on shore just south of Miami.

Our early morning press conference went well, but the information coming out of Florida had everyone worried. Larry was already on the phone trying to determine if Feed the Children's services were going to be needed. After the conference, we were taken to the airport where a luxurious MGM Grand jet was being readied for us. Our group of 22, including Liberty Records staff members and an Entertainment Tonight TV crew, found itself belted into leather recliners with four flight attendants eager to spoil us. Soon, we were airborne, winging our way to Oakland for the next meeting.

When we were finished there, we were shuttled back to the airplane so we could get to Chicago for another press gathering. Though we were late in arriving, the place was still packed with fans eager to ask Garth more questions. It was well after midnight when everyone got to bed, knowing we had to be in the lobby at 5:30 in the morning to catch a ride to the airport.

As we boarded the jet, we were greeted with warm moist towels with which to wipe our sleepy faces. Lox and bagels and other breakfast food had been pre-

pared for our quick trip to St. Louis. There, we were greeted with more excited fans and photographers.

Meanwhile in the Gulf of Mexico, hurricane Andrew was grinding its way into Louisiana. As the first pictures were just coming in from Florida, Larry Jones told us that trucks loaded with bottled water and other emergency supplies were already on their way.

From St. Louis we flew to Washington, DC, for the only outdoor event on the tour. It was hot and steamy in the park near the Potomac were Garth and Larry answered another round of questions. When we were done, we were limoed back to the plane for the last leg of our journey. Once again, the attendants

This page: Jane Pauley gets to "play" on the stage of the Grand Ole Opry after interviewing Garth (1992); facing page: Garth and Sandy introduce their first child, Taylor Mayne Pearl Brooks, to the world (1992).

met us with moist face towels. When we tried to decline them, thinking they would be hot, we were informed that these had been in the refrigerator. They knew exactly what we needed after boiling in the humidity. We were soon on our way to New York for one more press conference.

The next morning Larry Jones left the group and flew to Florida as the scope of the disaster became more obvious. Garth was left to handle a Good Morning America interview that had already been scheduled. His absence made the cause for which the funds were being raised very real. By the end of the

year, we knew that the seven city press tour was not in vain, and that Feed the Children was an organization deserving of the public's support. Beyond the Season sold over 2 million copies by Christmas, helping keep the trucks rolling to children and communities in need all over the country.

That fall, the CMA named Garth's album Ropin' the Wind as the Album of the Year and chose him as Entertainer of the Year for the second time. The combined sales of all his albums including the newest one, The Chase, were nearing the 30 million mark as 1992 came to an end.

But Garth also received one of his biggest disappointments that fall, when radio stations were reluctant to play his song "We Shall Be Free". Written from the heart after the Rodney King verdict lead to riots in Los Angeles at the same time The Academy of Country Music was presenting its award show, it meant a lot to him. Critics complained it was too preachy and way too gospel for their format. It stopped on the Billboard charts at twelve, lower than his first single "Much Too Young to Feel This Damn Old", which had made it to eight. Garth was beginning to get a little of the backlash that comes with fame.

When an artist makes it to the top, there's always someone who wants to shake the rope.

But the other three singles made it to number one in R & R and by 1999 The Chase had sold over 8 million copies. The song "We Shall Be Free" is one of the most popular with Garth's live audiences. Invariably,

the audience sings and sways like a gospel choir, totally involved in the song. Garth just smiles and sings along, like a choir leader.

This makes me think about Garth's fans. In 25 years I have been to more performances than I can count, some to shoot and some just to see. I've always been aware of who was in the audience with me, and not only how they reacted to the performer but how they acted, as well. After ten years of photographing his concerts and special occasions, I've discovered something Garth knows... his fans are among the nicest people in the world.

I've been down front with them on several occasions and talked with them as they stood in line to meet him. I've seen teenage cowboys act rowdy as they sang along on "Friends in Low Places", then take off their hats and hold their girlfriends close as they cried their way through "If Tomorrow Never Comes" and "The Dance". It is special, the way he connects with them. They care about each other. Scientists call that a symbiotic relationship. One cannot exist without the other.

This page: Garth waves at the audience in Chicago during the whirlwind tour to promote his Christmas album, Beyond The Season, and to raise money for Feed The Children (1992); facing page: During his concerts at Texas Stadium in Dallas, Garth lives up to his promise to perform face-to-face with the fans farthest from the stage by "flying" up to greet them (1993).

Garth's concerts continued to sell out in record time all over the country in 1993, setting attendances in the process. He developed a way to thwart ticket scalpers by adding concerts to fill the demand in a certain area. Instead of doing one night like most artists did, he would do three or four nights in a row, so everybody could get tickets. For a time, he didn't sell the first three rows, instead giving the tickets away to the folks in the nose-bleed section. At a concert in Knoxville, Tennessee, his parents went up to distribute the tickets and were met with skepticism, thinking this had to be a trick. Then someone recognized his mother, and the tickets were snatched up in no time. I talked to some of those fans as they came down front and they were overwhelmed with excitement. They never sat down, becoming part of the show instead of just concert-goers.

Garth also announced at Fanfair that he was going to do a series of shows in Dallas to film for a new television special. Called This is Garth Brooks, Too! , it immediately sold out Texas Stadium's 50,000 seat arena for three nights. They scheduled one more day to do some pickup shots, inviting audience members to come back for free, and packed the place again. At the press conference, he assured us that though the venue was huge, he would at some time be in the faces of the fans farthest away. This led to two months of speculation as to how he was going to do that. Would he use ramps, or be shot out of a cannon? In the great tradition of Harry Houdini, he had announced he would do the impossible, thus adding

to the excitement.

Sure enough, as he sang his newest single, "Ain't Going Down Till the Sun Comes Up", Garth rose up off the stage and into the lofty spaces of this big indoor facility and flew, with the help of invisible wires, to the back of the arena. I was standing up where the TV cameras ordinarily covered the Cowboys football games, so when he went by, he was directly out in front of me smiling and waving down at the audience. He floated to within feet of the folks in the upper balcony and sang directly to them, then he was reeled back over the stage and slowly lowered

down just in time for the ending of the song. It was so amazing to see, that I kept having to remind myself to take photos. Garth had lived up to his promise, and he did it with flare.

The co-writers of "Ain't Goin' Down", Kent Blazey and Kim Williams, told meat the #1 party that as they put together this complicated tongue-twisting roller coaster ride of a song, Garth never looked back at the words scribbled on the notepad. Just like the writing session, the song took off and never looked back. It broke R & R's records by entering the charts at twenty-five and rising to #1 in a matter of weeks. I

made a two song tape of it and Travis Tritt's version of "T-R-O-U-B-L-E", what I called a "crankin' tape", and proceeded to get a speeding ticket one night in the exact spot I'd gotten one to Restless Heart's "Wheels" several years before. When I was pulled over, the officer found me laughing as I handed him my license. "It's this damned country music", I said as I turned up the volume. When he realized what I meant, he laughed, too, then handed me the ticket.

That fall, Garth held a big party to recognize all of the people involved with the creation of his album, No Fences, which had exceeded the 10 million sales mark in just three years.. He chose to go back to the little shopping center north of Nashville, where he and Sandy had sold boots while he was trying to start a career. One by one, he handed out plaques to the Liberty Records staff, the songwriters, The Opry staff and many, many others involved in his success. He felt it very important to share the glory, knowing he didn't do it alone.

In 1994, Garth took his show on the road touring Europe and Australia. He was amazed that they, too, knew all the words to his songs, and his concerts in Ireland looked more like a rowdy pub scene as the audience sang louder than Garth. In the documentary of his tour, Trying to Rope the World, you can see the amazement on his face as they took over the show. He still calls them some of the most fun shows he's ever done.

That fall, Liberty Records released The Hits package at a gala party that also celebrated No Fences' exceeding 11 million in sales. The room was packed as he toasted everyone who'd made it possible. After the ceremony was over, Garth started signing autographs and posing for photos with friends that had lined up to greet him. About that time, recording legend Neil Diamond snuck into the room to offer his congratulations. Rather than barging past the line, he slipped into it, and snuck up on Garth.

When Garth looked up to greet the next well-wisher, he was surprised at who he saw. He whipped off his hat faster than Billy the Kid could pull out a Colt .45, and extended his hand, humbled by his attendance. Neil grinned at his surprise, as Garth called him "Mr. Diamond". When I asked Garth if he wanted to pose for a photo, he turned to the legendary superstar, and asked his permission. I'm please to say that "Mr. Diamond" was more than willing to have his picture made with this new superstar.

A few nights later, Garth celebrated Ropin' The Wind's 10 million sales mark on the stage of The Grand Old Opry. His Opry buddy, Johnny Russell, writer of the classic song "Act Naturally", a hit for Buck Owens and The Beatles, assisted The Recording Academy in presenting the award. Once again, as he accepted the multi-platinum plaque, he thanked everyone who'd helped him achieve this unprecedented landmark in an already amazing career. Two ten million-selling albums in a row, and they came from 16th Avenue in Nashville, Tennessee. Since then, The Hits

This page: At the party for the release of his album The Hits, Garth is surprised by one of his guests, the legendary Neil Diamond (1994); facing page: Garth dons a special suit before entering the CD mastering room at EMI's Recording Pressing plant in Jacksonville, Illinois (1995).

has joined the ten million club, recently named by the RIAA as a new category above platinum distinction, known as the Diamond Award. Pretty cool.

In 1995, Garth hit a plateau that few have ever achieved. The combined sales of his albums had passed the fifty million mark. To celebrate it, he went to a quiet little town named Jacksonville, Illinois, to the EMI Record Pressing plant, where all of his music had been manufactured. He wanted to thank the people who had done a magnificent of creating the final product that the people would buy somewhere in the world. If the tapes and CD's had sounded crappy, no one would've bought them.

I got to be part of this trip, and it was a wonderful education for me. I'd been to the old vinyl record pressing plants in Nashville several years before, so I

was getting to see how the industry had progressed. It occurred to me to ask one of the executives if other artists had ever visited them. He named one minor rock group, then pointed out that Garth had been there four times, "once before we knew who he was", he said with a smile.

I cannot say how enjoyable this trip was to me. We often hear about Washington's Beltway Mentality concerning the political needs of the citizens. Nashville sometimes has its own "Music Row Mentality" about what the listeners want to hear. I learned very quickly from these workers what they loved to hear. They loved to hear Garth Brooks, because they'd made what the radio played.

I want to point out to you that this is an industrial plant that runs three shifts a day. It had not shut

down for a minute in years. The employees of that plant had worked overtime through the Christmas holidays creating copies of "The Hits" that took him over the top. That day, I witnessed the whole production line stop for "a day off with Garth". He did not forget their sacrifice, and wanted them to know it.

During the formal part of the ceremony, a representative of The Chamber of Commerce in Jacksonville pointed out how many families there were in that community who could point to Garth's

success as their reason for their employment. I don't know if he'd thought of it that way before, as he bowed his head under his cowboy hat. His career was becoming a cottage industry that sustained the livelihoods of an ever increasing number of people.

He did know that the people he was honoring that day deserved the recognition for the work they'd put into his career, as well as, the perfect product they'd made for the other artists in the EMI Music family. It's nice that one of the stars stopped long enough to let them know how much they are appreciated. That afternoon, when I left with the Liberty Records crew and the TV cameras, Garth and Sandy and his parents were still there, wanting to meet them all. Another example of the symbiotic relationship.

Garth also took part in another interesting fundraiser in 1995. To help The Ronald McDonald House Foundation, he was one of four EMI artists, including Tina Turner, ___, and ___ to let them sell special CD collections through their restaurants to fund their charity. Garth's alone sold over three million copies.

Artist of the Decade

Garth started his "Thank You's" by thanking Stephanie Brown for introducing him to Bob Doyle. What he didn't tell you was that she was also his landlady for a short time, renting part of her Inglewood house to he and Sandy shortly after they moved to town. She also co-wrote "Burning

Bridges" which he included on Ropin' the Wind. She once told me that he came to her with this idea, but that she thought would be too cliched. Then he started singing the story about someone oiling the hinges like it was a favor, only to use their silence as a way to sneak out. She was struck by his unique approach to an old idea, so they finished the song. She was also struck by his determination to make the song work. Maybe that's why she felt secure in sending him to Bob. He never forgot her help.

When Garth wanted to split The Academy of Country Music's Artist of the Decade Award with George Strait and Reba McEntire, it made perfect sense to me. Consistently, throughout their careers, they have paid attention to their audiences. Just ask my mother about George Strait, he can do no wrong. Personally, since 1977, I've watched Reba's way of making a career, and she's done everything she can to do it right. Both of them are artists who listen to their fans and have made sure the music business did the same. They've worked very hard to miss such a recognition just because there's only one every decade. Garth knows what they've done and let us know this as he accepted this award. Then again, maybe that's part of the reason he deserved to receive it. ▧

8 | THE NEXT GENERATION

Clockwise from top left: Redmon & Vale; Matt King; Andy Griggs with Brett Jones; Deryl Dodd; Linda Davis with producer Wally Wilson; Lisa Angelle with Louis Anderson; Chalee Tennison; center: Montgomery Gentry with James "Bo" Garrett.

People often ask me who I enjoy photographing the most. With all the choices I've had in twenty-five years, the answer is still quite easy: It's the new kids who are just breaking into the business. From Reba McEntire and Steve Wariner in the 1970s through Kathy Mattea, Alan Jackson and Garth Brooks in the 1980s, and into the 1990s with Jo Dee Messina, the Wilkinsons and Tim McGraw, I have always gotten a kick out of shooting the freshmen.

Those first steps they take as they climb the musical ladder of success are always the most interesting. From the contract signings and showcases to their first studio sessions or Fanfair appearances, these young artists always seem to be amazed that they're really here. Sometimes they're terrified, fearing that somehow it'll all fall apart at the last minute, but usually they are bubbling over with excitement. Their innocence is refreshing in this world of professionals.

In 1999, I saw a number of new artists get their start in Nashville. A new label, DreamWorks, has opened the door to a career for young Jessica Andrews and Redmon & Vale. Brad Paisley and Sherrie Austin have been given a chance at Arista Records. South Sixty-Five and Matt King have been added to the roster at Atlantic Records. Virgin Records Nashville has just introduced us to their first country act, Julie Reeves.

Montgomery/Gentry and Deryl Dodd are among the new artists being nurtured by Sony Music. Trini Triggs and Shane McAnally are attempting to take advantage of the break given them by Curb Records. Asylum Records has placed their hopes on new artists like Chalee Tennison and Monte Warden and Lila McCann. Rebecca Lynn Howard, Alecia Eliott and Chely Wright have recently been added to MCA's stable of artists. Mercury Records believes they have a winner with Shane Minor. Lyric Street has recently released the first single on their new act, SHeDAISY, and Vince Gill is finishing his first production duties for them with his former backup vocalist, Sonya Isaacs.

RCA Label Group has already had great success with Sara Evans and Andy Griggs, who had their first number-one records in 1999. Another RCA artist, Jason Sellers, is bubbling just under the surface with a new album to share with the public. Capitol Records is betting on Garth Brooks former band member Ty England and contemporary Christian artist Susan Ashton to make it in country music. The list goes on and on.

Who out of this group of new performers will make it? Only time will tell. I've learned that the decision is not up to me—it's up to the fans to choose which ones have a future in this town. My job to make sure we have photos of their baby steps as they toddle into the music business, before the hard knocks of the business harden them into seasoned performers or dash their career hopes. I'll always enjoy working with Nashville's next generation. They are the future of country music.

This page, clockwise from top left: Trini Triggs; Shane Minor; Shane McAnally; Alecia Elliott with George Strait; Rebecca Lynn Howard; Jason Sellers with producer Walt Aldridge; Jessica Andrews with Brenda Lee; center: Ty England.
Facing page: Chely Wright; Brad Paisley; Lila McCann; Sherrie Austin; South Sixty Five; Monte Warden; center: Beverly Ellis.

257

Clockwise from top left: Chad Brock and Sara Evans; Keith Urban with Hip-Hop producer Stevie J; Jeff Carson; Kenny Chesney with songwriters Tony Mullins and Wendell Mobley; Julie Reeves; The Wilkinsons (father, Steve and children Amanda and Tyler with mom, Chris and younger sister Kiaya); The Lynns, Susan Ashton with Jim Brickman.